Quick & Painless Business Writing

Quick & Painless Business Writing

An Essential Guide to Clear and Powerful Communication

by Susan F. Benjamin

CAREER
PRESS

Franklin Lakes, NJ

Quick and Painless Business Writing
EDITED BY KARA REYNOLDS
TYPESET BY ASTRID DERIDDER
Cover design by Rob Johnson/Johnson Design
Printed in the U.S.A. by Book-mart Press

To order this title, please call toll-free 1-800-CAREER-1 (NJ
and Canada: 201-848-0310) to order using VISA or MasterCard,
or for further information on books from Career Press.

The Career Press, Inc., 3 Tice Road, PO Box 687,
Franklin Lakes, NJ 07417
www.careerpress.com

Library of Congress Cataloging-in-Publication Data

Benjamin, Susan, 1957-
Quick and painless business writing : an essential guide to
clear and powerful communication / by Susan F. Benjamin.
    p. cm.
    Includes index.
    ISBN-13: 978-1-56414-900-8
    ISBN-10: 1-56414-900-5
    1. Business writing. I. Title.

HF5718.3.B458 2007
651.7'4--dc22

                                                    2006020299

Dedication

To Dan and Adam, the smartest, funniest guys I know.
Thanks for helping me tap the energy and humor in my own voice.

Acknowledgments

Writing a book is never easy. Okay, actually, writing this book *was* easy, but who wants to start an acknowledgment page that way? So, I want to acknowledge *not* the people who helped me trudge through the misery of the writing process, but those who made it possible for me to write—and delight in—this book.

First, my agent. Let me tell you, every good writer (and every bad writer for that matter) needs a good agent. And Grace Freedson's the best. She's available, interested, and willing to drink a glass of wine with her author even when better judgment tells her not to. More than an agent, she's a dream-maker and friend.

But even with a great agent, you still need content. That's where my clients come in. So big thanks to the National Geospatial Intelligence Agency University, The Missile Defense Agency, The Office of Personal Management, Fleishman-Hillard, The Carnegie

Mellon Executive Program, and, of course, Liberty Mutual Group, among others. Every seminar I taught and project I worked on was its own learning experience.

Special thanks to everyone in the Plain Language Initiative under Clinton-Gore: Annetta Cheek, Bill Foster, Kate Blunt, and many others; and to those who trusted me to research language strategies, conduct focus groups, and unearth something new: Ellen Tunstall, Janice Seimsen, and Steve Sullivan. Many of the lessons I learned in overseeing these projects are in this book.

Also big thanks to Rick Frishman for his referrals and advice, Josh Stellar for the emergency care on my computer just before deadline, and my proofer Libby Howard—ever ready with a correction and a joke—who doubtless has read and corrected this very line.

Of course, fortifying the writer's life are all the people who say things like: "How's the book going?" which I take as encouragement, and "Don't worry, I'll take your son for the afternoon while you work." In particular, Kathryn Stellar, Lissa and Garth Jansen, Rose McKee, and at the old home front, Margie Green and Susan Erony for their goodwill and good wishes. And finally, thanks to Kitty Clark, modern dance teacher, for showing me my body can do more than sit in front of a keyboard.

Contents

The Quick, Painless, and Indispensable Introduction   11

Section I: Why Quick? Why Painless? Why Not?

Chapter 1: Five No-Worry Reality Checks   19

Section II: Word Use—No Pain, All Gain

Chapter 2: Ouchless Nouns   33

Chapter 3: Noun Accomplices: Articles,
Pronouns, and Adjectives   51

Chapter 4: Verbs: The Power Words   65

Chapter 5: Glue Words   89

Chapter 6: Sentence Savvy   99

Section III: Quick, Painless, and Plain: Almost All You Need to Know About Style

Chapter 7: Plain Language Primer: So What Are The Big Guys Afraid Of?   113

Chapter 8: Why the Active Voice Isn't, and a Few Words About Being Concise   121

Chapter 9: Reader-Focus: Bowing to the King and Queen of the Universe   139

Chapter 10: The Truth About Tone, Damn It!   157

Section IV: Cohesive Structure: Keeping It Together

Chapter 11: Seducing, Spinning, and Sedating: All About Structure   173

Chapter 12: The Paragraph: On Closer Inspection   185

Chapter 13: The End   211

Index   215

About the Author   221

Introduction

Why Quick and Painless?

The Six Golden Rules of Writing:
Read, read, read and write, write, write.
—Ernest Gains

So why "Quick and Painless" business writing? Better to ask why *not*. Granted, you'd probably prefer drinking a Bloody Mary on a Sunday afternoon than writing a report in your cubicle—or sunny home office for that matter—but all things considered, writing isn't the worst (or hardest) job in the world. In fact, you might actually enjoy it. Plenty of people do.

To get there, though, you need to extricate all that hurts and slows you down. You see, throughout your life, you've been overdosing on advice, ranging from practical (but distracting) to maddening, about the written word. Lessons from even your most beloved teachers probably included too many rules to possibly remember, including when to use "I" or "me," "may" or "can," and why certain words—even those words that felt as comfortable as in worn-in sneakers—were taboo.

To get perspective, you probably turned to books about writing. And there are LOTS to choose from. Frankly, I wish I'd written some of them, especially Strunk and White's classic, *The Elements of Style*. It sold a gazillion copies and reads like a good novel—an interesting, light style. And yes, many of those books do contain useful information.

There's only one problem: None of those how-tos can really help you write. They can give you guidance, sure, but how about a sense of voice? Or direction for how to best heal your writing ills and maximize your strengths? Think about writing as an athletic event and you know what I mean. Did Tiger Woods learn to play golf from a manual? Did Mohammad Ali become a great boxer by memorizing rules? No—they figured out how to work from their natural abilities. To overcome obstacles. And to adapt their style, depending on the environment, the opposition, and what they hoped to achieve.

So, before you turn the pages of *Quick and Painless Business Writing*, read the following adages. They'll help you maximize the information that follows—some of it reminiscent of lessons past, and much of it entirely new. And do the exercises that you'll find in every chapter. They won't take long and will help you experience immediate results. In the process, you'll find writing isn't just quick and painless—it's quick and satisfying.

Pre-nitty-gritty Adages

Take a one-step-at-a-time approach. As we go through each of these chapters, from nouns to cohesive structure, check your writing. How does it measure up? Are you strong in one particular area? If so, keep it up. If not, identify that problem—be it wordiness, sentence structure foibles, or anemic verbs. Then, focus on correcting that problem every time you write until you overcome it. Then move on to the next requirement. And give yourself a hand: You learned something and got your money's worth from this book.

Think strategy. Sure, follow the rules of writing, the ones you learned in high school, college, and business-writing classes...unless they seem impractical, outdated, or unnecessary. Then, think strategy. Think your sentence sounds more natural with a pre-position at the end? Go ahead, if the situation's informal and your reader won't object. Want to tell a joke? If you're drafting regulations, better not. But if you're writing marketing material or an e-mail to a close colleague, all the better.

Get help. Lots of help. Professional writers, including *New York Times* journalists and Pulitzer Prize–winning novelists, have a squad of professionals giving feedback on all they write. As for me, I have an editor, agent, book coach, proofreader, and assorted content experts full of ample supplies of feedback. Usually, they comment on my genius and offer heaps of praise. I'm kidding; I've experienced waves of negatives. When they're constructive, I wallow in them a while, and then do what they suggest. When they're uselessly critical, I swim right past them. It's either that or drown.

So, get help, only get the *right* help. Here are some people to depend on:

◆ **Peer editors.** These coworkers can review your material—and hopefully you'll review theirs. As with any good relationship, you and your peers should have different strengths and weaknesses. Have problems with sentence structure? Then find someone who has mastered this aspect of writing, but is weak in areas where you excel. Then, give him or her feedback in return.

◆ **Your manager.** Managers can be iffy. Some have great insights, while others remain stuck in archaic styles of writing. Besides, they decide whether you'll get a raise, a promotion, or a transfer. So do you really want to appear vulnerable? If your manager gives you feedback anyway, learn more. What are the reasons for the changes he or she suggested? And what negative patterns can the two of you find and avoid in the future?

◆ **Professional trainers and coaches.** You may find great sources of feedback through training centers at your company or through adult education programs. The instructors will work with you in one-on-one sessions and provide confidential and invaluable insights. Call around and find out where and when. And don't forget to contact the English department at your local college. Graduate students, and even some professors, are usually willing to help for a manageable fee.

Read. Every day. It's imperative. Consciously or not, you imitate the styles of the documents you read. No matter how many writing classes you take or writing workbooks you open, you *still* need to read. You don't have to read highbrow literature: in fact, you don't *want* to read highbrow literature. It will slow down your style. Instead, read what you enjoy. Here are some ideas:

◆ **Read newspapers and magazines.** Amazingly, according to Journalism.org's annual *State of the News Media* report in 2004, only slightly more than half the population reads hardcopy newspapers, yet newspapers offer up some of the best writing around. It's usually fast and interesting—just the way you like it. Want to read *The Wall Street Journal*? Go ahead. But don't feel embarrassed if you prefer to indulge in your local tabloid. Regardless, an article over coffee in the morning will fortify your style for the day.

◆ **Read books.** I know this sounds obvious, but many people don't read them. In fact, the average American only reads *one* book a year—usually in summer for some "sea 'n' sun" entertainment. Yet they're the greatest influence imaginable on your writing. You stay immersed in the book's language for a long time, relaxing and enjoying the experience, much like soaking in a hot tub. You'll flow from chapter to chapter, witnessing how the author's ideas come together. As for the (in)famous literary novels? As I said, don't reach for Russian tragedies if your heart craves true romance.

- ◆ **Read workplace documents with caution.** Yes, you have to read workplace documents. But beware: read these and nothing else, and you unconsciously start duplicating the style. Depending on the document, it may be as interesting and provocative as the ingredients on a can of paint.

- ◆ **Remember the fun factor.** So we've established that most people don't read for pleasure. But why? My guess is people read for the wrong reasons. Most think books are good for them. Books will make them better people, somehow. Stronger people. Healthier people. Reasons why you might, say, eat green, leafy vegetables. That's true, of course, books *are* good for you. The real reasons to read and keep on reading, though: it's fun, lasts far longer than a movie, and is more intensive than Web surfing. Oh—and books and magazines are easier to carry around than a television set.

Practice makes perfect. With writing, as with sports, you only improve by doing. And doing. And doing. And getting better as you go. So while cruising through this workbook you'll see suggested exercises. They're marked "Q&P Break." Stop, go to the computer, and go ahead. Don't worry—these exercises won't take hours each. In fact, they work similar to the drip method of irrigation: By doing small amounts every day, your style will be fresh and fertile. Many have a high usability factor, too, meaning you can actually write and rewrite copy for work.

Anything else?

You'll learn lots of things formally and informally as we go along, such as how to place words strategically, to maximize the power of your message, and the optimal approach to using sentence rhythms. You'll even learn to *read* other people's documents differently—especially when their message is unclear or poorly written.

So sit back, relax, grab a drink and a pen and paper, and let's get started.

Section I

Why Quick? Why Painless? Why Not?

Chapter 1
Five No-Worry Reality Checks

Reality Check #1: The Response

Let's start with the Mother of All Reality Checks—the ultimate reason you write at work. But first, answer this question: Why write at work? Don't think about your answer—just respond from your gut. A few words will do. Ready? What's your answer?

If you're like most of the tens of thousands of people I've trained over the years, it probably was: "To communicate," or "To send information," or something like that. Actually, writing to communicate is the job of newspapers and magazines. People read them to get information, pass the time, sip a Mimosa on a Sunday morning, and flip through the pages of the Sunday edition.

In the business world, you write to get a response. Writing a proposal? You want the reader to sign on the dotted line. Sending an e-mail asking for material? You want the material, but that's not all. You want the material now, today, right away. Not, say, after two or three phone calls or follow-up e-mails. Writing a job announcement? Sure, you want people to apply. But you want the *right* people to apply, and send you the right information when they do. That means, of course, you *don't* want the wrong people to apply and have to sift through endless incorrect applications. You know the drill.

The importance of getting the right response is no small matter. In fact, it affects just about everything in your business. Let's look at that e-mail I mentioned a moment ago. Here's how it goes:

Hypothetical e-mail scenario: You're writing a report. Since this is hypothetical, I'm tempted to say the report was for a client and included recommendations that would help them immeasurably and bring you a $2.2 million contract. But your e-mail is probably the more run-of-the-mill variety, such as you and your team are writing a report to help your boss determine the next steps for a project and you need information from another department.

What happened: You sent the e-mail telling your associate in that other department about the project, what you needed, why, and when.

What happened next: Nothing. So you e-mailed again.

And then? Nothing. Still nothing. So you called to remind them.

And: They still didn't respond, so you found someone else to send the e-mail. Or: They did respond, but you didn't get everything you wanted. Or: They did respond, only it was late. Or...lots of other possibilities.

Naturally, the cost of this delay adds up. There's your time spent in e-mailing and calling the person. Then, there's the time of others on your team who can't move forward with their contribution to the report until they have the missing information. And at long last, there's the valuable time of that back-up person you contact since the original (still!) didn't respond. Plus the stop-and-go time of delaying various aspects of the report and the project, which is on hold since your boss didn't get the report...Now, multiply this by 10 or even 20 unopened or unanswered e-mails and...well...you know where I'm going.

Getting the Wrong Response?

Getting the wrong response? Then these scenarios will sound familiar:

◆ If you're sending job announcements, you probably get the wrong people applying for the wrong job. Or maybe the right people are applying but they're sending the wrong documents.

◆ If you're writing customer service letters, customers call having *no idea* why you didn't refund their $12.50 even though you explained it, in detail, for three paragraphs.

◆ If you write technology instructions and people call, confused about how to use the software, even though you used a clear chronological approach that would make Steven Spielberg weep.

◆ If you send e-mails asking for information and get no reply. Yet again.

Quick Q&P Break

Write a list of the most common documents you have to write. They can be everything from e-mails announcing meetings through performance reviews of difficult employees to your average invitation. Then write the response you want to get in return. But don't be simplistic. Tell all. Then, hold on to that list—and apply the ideas in this book to ensure you get the kind of response you had in mind.

Reality Check #2: Your Reader: A Surprise Profile

To get the right response, you must know your reader, and trust me, today's reader is a creature unto itself. I'm just old enough to look back on the good old days of typewriters, cable-less TV, and a virtuous reality. *Leave It to Beaver* showed a lifestyle we all aspired to, and the pace of life was more measured...slower. Back then, people read letters, memos, and other messages from the first line to the last, sometimes rereading them just to make sure. No message was ever shorter than three or four paragraphs—each, at least in the writer's opinion, chock-full of attention-worthy information.

Today, the reader is even *more* dependent on the written word, what with the prevalence of Websites, e-mails, and the wonder of Blackberries, yet they're more averse to reading. Your message must reach them instantly, more like a transfusion of data than a process of passing along information one paragraph at a time. Even the graying Baby Boomers want Superman-style language: faster than a speeding bullet and more powerful than a locomotive. Every opening line, every header, every *word* must convince them to read and keep on reading.

As for the length and duration of their reading habits, think the reader slowly moves from your opening line to the end of your document? Forget it. They read the beginning...maybe, then skim, jump to another section, call their pal and arrange to go out for a beer after work, then return to the document...or not. Got a meeting to go to—bye.

Fast Facts About Your Reader
Every Business Writer Should Know...

Your Readers:

◆ Watch anywhere from four to six hours of television a day...although some say more.

◆ Read one book a year—usually in the summer.

◆ Get their news in sound-bite speed online and on the tube: Only a little more than 50 percent read hardcopy newspapers.

◆ Decide whether they like a Website in less time than it takes to blink an eye.

◆ Decide whether they like other print messages in only two or three words.

◆ Read openings, sometimes closings, and very little of the middle of most business documents.

◆ Retain far more of what they *read* than what they hear.

Reality Check #3: Your Education

Now, we get to the grizzly part of this chapter: your education. Those lessons from your high school, college, and even business school teachers who gave you counterproductive information. Okay—it wasn't *all* counterproductive, but did it help you reach today's wildly impatient reader?

I'm sure you remember the English class experience well. I do: Some 30-odd years later, I still recall Forest Grove Junior High School. The students, naturally, suffered from hormone overload and mass-scale ADHD (Attention Deficit Hyperactivity Disorder). And controlling this wayward mob were grown-ups such as Miss Ferguson, my 7th grade English teacher.

Miss Ferguson opened her teacher's guidebook every day and doled out rules, which we were expected to memorize. Mostly we learned the names of words, such as "complete predicate," "sub-junctive," and that sort of thing, as well as the intricacies of commas. Ask a question, and Miss Ferguson flipped the page of her teacher's guidebook until she found the answer and read it aloud. Or she did one of those "What do you think?" routines, in which the teacher pauses, then looks you straight in the face and says: "What do you think?" Or: "You should know this by now. Look up the answer and get back to us."

Naturally, you thought the teacher was forcing you to learn. Activating your lazy mind. Making you THINK FOR YOURSELF. Nope. I taught college students for 14 years and I did the same thing. Someone asked an impossible question and rather than answer it for the ten-thousandth time in your career, get off-track in the schedule, or admit the unthinkable and say: "I have absolutely *no* idea," I said: "What do you think?" So did plenty of my colleagues. Ditto for Miss Ferguson.

Anyway, in between this memorize-rules approach, we actually *did* write. And what we wrote...I'm sure you remember well. Those five-paragraph essays that began: "In the following, I am going to discuss ..." The next three paragraphs discussed those same topics, until the conclusion, where we told the reader: "In summary, I have discussed..." as if the reader suffered from acute short-term memory loss and we needed to help them along. This, as you'll see later in this book, is a huge deficit when addressing a reader who wants the message *now* and wants everything that follows to be new, fresh, and useful.

Then there were the page requirements. Such as: write three to five pages. So you get to page two and have nothing else to say. At least one full page (and nothing to say) to go. The panic sets in like an intravenous shot of Red Bull, so you start cramming the sheet with as many extra words as possible. And before you know it, you have a wordiness problem. A good grade, but a wordiness problem.

Miss Ferguson tried, I'm sure. And I'm sure she wanted us to be good writers or good students or good *something*. Only Miss Ferguson, and all the Miss Fergusons across the country, had three strikes against them. Here goes:

Strike One: The Ivory Tower Problem

They don't call schools the "ivory tower" for nothing—even when they're filled with hormonally overcharged adolescents. The school–reality connection *can* be vague. Let's get back to the five-paragraph essays we mentioned a moment ago. They formed the basis of your writing style, yet hardly prepared you for real-life communications. How many times have you seen an essay in real life? In the newspaper? At work? Has your customer, boss, or board of directors ever required an *essay* about your project? As for the standardized paragraph—you remember, right? With the topic sentence, body, and concluding sentence? Non-existent. We could go on and on...and in this book, we probably will. But let's move on for now.

Strike Two: Poor Training

Just last night I had dinner with a woman who received her Ph.D. in philosophy. This tells you two things: (1) She's smart.

(2) She's not entirely practical. But that's okay. We have too many practical people running around anyway. And what does this woman with a Ph.D. in philosophy do for a living? Why, she teaches *writing*.

You may wonder why a Ph.D. in philosophy—a field of study *not* known to be especially clear and succinct—is teaching writing. I'm not sure, actually. But she's not alone. Plenty of Composition 101 teachers in universities everywhere aren't writers but graduate students with a work-study arrangement with the school. Or teachers who specialize in other things. Or struggling poets who know nothing about business writing but need to make a buck. As for high school? They're teachers. Not, say, writers or linguists or even businesspeople with substantial experience with writing at work. In fact, unless you entered programs specifically designed for writers, your teachers probably knew as much about business writing as you did.

Strike Three: Grammar Rules Misconceptions

Most teachers—not to mention bosses and reviewers—believe that grammar rules are scientific facts. Follow them—or you'll implode. In reality, the grammar "rules" change just as everything else—cars, clothing, and music. Granted, you may not like the new style, but there's no turning back. And this leads us to the all important Reality Check #4: Who Needs Grammar Rules?

Q&P Break: Tell-All

Remember any outrageous English class lessons? Have a teacher who struck a nerve—good or bad? Have a funny, sad, or otherwise interesting story about English class? Now's your chance to share it. Just get on *www.quickandpainlessbusinesswriting.com* and send it along. I'll take a look, and quite possibly, post.

Reality Check #4: Who Needs Grammar Rules?

How many times have you paused, mid-speech, wondering whether you should say "I" or "me"? How many sentences have you reordered so you don't get stuck with a preposition hanging at the end? How many times have you paused, just short of using "who"...or was that "whom"?

Why the pause? The trepidation? The out-and-out fear about getting it wrong? Because grammar rules are a litmus test for intelligence. People endlessly make accusations such as: "He's a real idiot...you should see how he writes!" Or, "Didn't this guy make it through high school?" when a poorly conceived sentence rears its ugly misplaced modifiers.

Even worse, some people consider grammar rules to be moral imperatives. Bad writing = bad person. The degree of badness equals the degree of the grammatical flaw. A sentence with a split infinitive, such as "We are going *to quickly finish* that project and go home for lunch" equals the moral equivalent of a deliberately timed-out parking meter. But a sentence with "ain't"? The grammatical equivalent to murder.

To help free you from the weight of those beliefs, and show you the path to better writing, here are some grammar facts you should know.

The Grammar Gene

Many linguists attribute grammar to a gene that's in all of us. The idea of the so-called grammar gene goes something like this: If you put a bunch of babies on an island and raise them without any language at all—not *Sesame Street*; Peter, Paul and Mary; or adoring compliments from elderly aunts—they would find their own means of communicating. This ability is encoded in them. Maybe they'd use hand gestures, grunts, or other sounds. But eventually, a pattern would evolve so they could articulate their needs. And this pattern would become their grammatical system.

There's Grammar, and Then There's Grammar

The word "grammar," which we use with such reckless abandon in English classes and out, actually refers to two separate things: grammar and usage. By "grammar" we mean the consistency of language. "The printer don't gets no ink high so paper the it don't look good no," is not grammatical by anyone's standards. Then there's "usage"—which plenty of people *mistake* for grammar. It changes with the times—and unless you change with it, your writing will be as useful as the phonograph. If you're unsure about what I mean, try reading Shakespeare, the Declaration of Independence, or a copy of *Harper's Magazine* from 1890.

So what has made these rules change? And which ones have changed, exactly? Keep reading...

Language Fashion and Flair

You'd be amazed at the forces that have shaped the English language: wars, invasions, economic conditions, political strife...in fact, make a movie about the subject and you'd have a blockbuster that could make a Steven Seagal action flick look like Disney's Donald Duck.

More recent influences include immigration—which has injected our language with lots of new and delicious-sounding words—and the Web, e-mails, Blackberries, and other electronic media. Everything from sentences to paragraphs must be short, short, short, with plenty of variety and Web space. Full sentences? Sure—but not always. In fact, look back a few words and you'll see I didn't use them. Highly formal and businesslike tone for *anything* leaving your office? Only if you're treating insomnia.

Here are some other changes:

The Rule: Never end a sentence with a preposition. Instead, flip the wording around so it sounds unnatural but reassuringly correct. So instead of saying "Where did this mess come from?" You say: "How did this mess come about?" Nope, preposition there too. Hmm. Oh, I know: "How did this mess evolve?" Or: "From where did this mess come?"

The Reality: Writing something for older readers or those from a traditional background? Then cover your bases and stick with the rule. But if you need to send a quick message to a colleague, go ahead, indulge. It's okay. "Where did this mess come from?" works when the atmosphere is informal.

The Rule: Say "who" when you're addressing the subject and "whom" when you're addressing the object.

The Reality: If you have no idea what I'm talking about, don't worry. This is the "out" column, and it won't matter anyway. In fact, erase "whom" from your mind in sentences like: "To whom does this beverage belong?" Your reader will probably think a British butler is asking the question.

The Rule: Don't use two negatives back to back, as in: I am not anti-French. The reasoning goes something like two negatives cancel each other out, so you end up with a positive.

The Reality: Look, there are no greater language snobs than the French. I'm not anti-French; it's just true. And they get to use double negatives, as in: Je n'ai sais pas (meaning "I don't know"—the "n'" and "pas" are both negatives). So why can't we?

The Rule: Don't split an infinitive. This is an infinitive: "To cram." This is a split infinitive: "To quickly cram for the CPA certification test." As far as I know, CPAs aren't known to cram in the first place—except at tax time. Normally, they calculate.

The Reality: Just about everyone learned they shouldn't split infinitives but practically no one knew what a split infinitive was and they kept doing it anyway. Besides, *Star Trek* took care of that. Who would argue that the un-split infinitive of "To go boldly where no man has gone..." sounds better than the original, hopelessly split version: "To boldly go where no man has gone..."?

Q&P Break

It isn't just the rules that have changed. It's the words themselves—the spelling, the meaning, which ones are acceptable as Standard English, and which ones are not. To make matters worse, style guides and dictionaries vary in their opinions. So what's a conscientious writer like you to do?

A few things: First, look through your bookshelves. Have an old dictionary you cling to for insights, clarity, and wisdom? Why, the very same dictionary your father used, and his father before that? Oh, and possibly your mother and grandmother? Toss it. Then get an updated edition and use that. Second, get a new edition every five or 10 years. Third, if your organization uses a particular guide, whether *The Associated Press Stylebook* or *The Chicago Manual of Style*, follow that. And make sure the company's version is updated as well.

Grammar Mavens: Upholders of the Writing Truth

We've now established that language rules change. Your readers' expectations also change. Unfortunately, as we mentioned, business-writing rules don't; the old and ineffective ways lingering on and on. Don't believe me? Try reading a policy manual. Or how about a regulation? Even the best documents sound as lively as a Buckingham Palace guard.

But deviate from this archaic style? Slip a "but" in the beginning of your sentence? Now you're getting dangerously close to the realm of Bad Writing, even if it sounds perfectly normal and good. Says who? Say the watchdogs of language, the Homeland Security of the Mother Tongue. In language circles, they're known as "Grammar Mavens." They shriek about deteriorating language and are willing to gouge your eyes out over a split infinitive. They insist you follow the Rules and any deviation from what they used in 1912 is tantamount to heresy.

At work, they're the reviewers, bosses, clients, and lawyers who insist on red-marking your document to death or twisting perfectly reasonable text into boring dribble. They exhaust you. Humiliate you. And take up your valuable time on non-valuable changes.

So how do you address these individuals? See Reality Check #5.

Reality Check #5: Let Logic Prevail

Let's face it: The business world isn't exactly a breeding ground for anarchy—even in the word-use realm. So experimentation is out. Logic and strategy are in. Here are two situations that prove the point.

Situation: Say your reviewer or boss insists on a lengthy preamble that no one will read but is critical because...well, they don't say why. No one ever says. Anyway, here are the choices.

Bad choice: Forget it. Do what you want. Cut that paragraph and when your boss demands you put it back in, tell her forget it. She knows nothing about the subject and should take a good writing class before dispensing idiotic rules.

Sound, logical choice: Explain that you read a book that advises against using long introductions because the reader wants the point right away. Try to reason with her—change her mind. Hopefully, she'll say yes.

Situation: Your boss insists you use jargon that's hard for insiders to understand—and impossible for everyone else. Even worse, your boss insists for legal reasons, as in: "If you don't use this language we could have a lawsuit on our hands."

Bad choice: Say: "That's nonsense" or worse. Then do what you want because, really, it *is* nonsense, or worse.

Sound, logical choice: Contact someone in your legal department and let your boss know he or she said it's alright. If you risk alienating your boss in the process, then keep the jargon...but slip in a more natural definition right next to it.

Q&P Sound and Logical Reminder

Of course, your boss or reviewer might be right. Maybe your message is convoluted. Painfully slow. Or hopelessly unfocused. But how do you know? Think the comment through, make sure you understand it, and if not, get a second opinion. Don't miss a chance to let your style grow.

Section II
Word Use—No Pain, All Gain

Chapter 2
Ouchless Nouns

When Do We Diagram Sentences? A Flashback

Back in 7th grade, I longed to become a great poet. Either that or an Oscar-winning actress, or a rock star like Janis Joplin (minus the heroin addiction). But then, didn't we all? I loved writing, reading, talking...just about anything involving words. But diagramming sentences? I remember sitting in Miss Ferguson's English class, my bowels knotting up in horror as I tried to draw those silly lines over those silly words, which made as much sense to me, an aspiring *poet*, as astrophysics.

Fortunately, instinct told me diagramming sentences was *not* about writing—in fact, *not* about communications at all. It was about...diagramming sentences. So I continued writing undeterred.

Unfortunately, Miss Ferguson's instinct *didn't* relay the same message and I got an unmentionably low grade in the course.

Nouns: All About Them

Nouns were probably your favorite words in junior high school—perhaps they're your favorite words now. They're easy to recognize—they name things—and even easier to use, unlike the more complex and demanding verbs. Here's a sample of some nouns in case you've forgotten:

Noun Reminder Cheat Sheet

school	Tom's Garage	counter-report
ferry	bus	listening device
rings	FBI	Long Island
candle	dog	Joe's Bar 'n' Grille
poodle	report	German Shepherd
money	nickels	Miss Ferguson
spy	fingernails	Betty's Nail Boutique

Let's start with the actor: whoever or whatever did the action. The actor reigns as the alpha of the word-use kingdom: It's the leader of the pack; first in the sentence. Or should be, anyway. To identify the actor, take this little test.

Step 1: Find a pencil or pen and a piece of paper. Don't bother booting up your computer; this will be quick.

Step 2: Look up. Write down the first thing you see. For example, I see a candle. So I'll write: "candle." This isn't rocket science, but it sure beats diagramming sentences, right? Anyway, whatever you wrote is your noun.

Step 3: What is your noun doing? My noun flickers. So I would say: "The candle flickers." Naturally, "flickers" is the verb.

Every sentence needs to have an actor: someone or something doing the action. This isn't a grammar rule—it's physics. If something happens, something or someone must *make* it happen. Think about it. Even the *wind* must blow the air around.

Second in the equality list is what we'll call the beta noun—aka the "object" of your sentence. Forget the word "object." It makes everything too confusing. Still important, but second in the pack. The beta noun receives the action—sometimes it appears in the sentence; sometimes it doesn't. For example, in "The candle flickers..." no beta noun is necessary. The candle flickers, that's all. Of course, I could say: "The candle flickers in my eye," and now the beta noun is "eye." Here are a few more examples:

◆ *The candle flickers across the room.*

◆ *The candle flickers inside my mind.*

◆ *The candle flickers, creating shadows.*

The Question You're Dying to Ask!

Q. Can you have more than one actor in the sentence?
A. Certainly—if you have more than one action.

Q. Can you give me an example?
A. Of course. I'll give you several.

Example 1: *Susan steadied the candle as Sammy the cat ran away.* (Actors: Susan and Sammy.)

Example 2: *Susan thinks the candle smells like evergreens.* (Actors: Susan and candle.)

Example 3: *Dan, Susan's husband, thinks the candle smells like deodorant and usually blows it out.* (Actors: Dan, definitely Dan, and candle.)

The Passive Voice

Doubtless, you've heard about the passive voice. Most people have. Sadly, most people also have high-level anxiety about the passive voice and can't tell the difference between a passive and active sentence. I'm not sure why. It could be because the terms "passive," "active," and "voice" have a vague to nonexistent connection to what they really mean.

The idea is very simple: Make sure the alpha noun holds its rightful place in the sentence, and you get the active voice. Disturb the arrangement, and you get the passive. I wish it were more complicated; then I, and other communications experts, would seem like pure geniuses, but alas, that's about it.

So here's what happens. Sometimes, when you're busy writing, you may forget to put the all-important actor in the sentence. The reader has no idea *who* did the action and the thought is incomplete. So you might end up saying:

◆ "The candle was almost knocked over." We already know who almost knocked over the candle...that would be Sammy, the cat—but the sentence should say so.

◆ "The phone call was never made no matter what George said." We can assume George never made the phone call...although we can't be sure.

◆ "Mistakes were made." This is a favorite of politicians—you've probably seen it hundreds of times. In this case, we *know* who made the mistake: the politician, but we're supposed to be fooled by the omission.

In other cases, the actor winds up at the end of the sentence and you end up with messy sentences similar to this one:

The candle was immediately steadied by me.

Or this one, from a politician:

Lies were spread by unknown members of my administration.

Even worse, some sentences contain both mistakes, and end up looking like this:

> *Lies were spread by unknown members of my administration and the culprit will be found and disciplined accordingly.*

Sounds familiar, right? The rewrite *should* look like this:

> *Members of my administration spread lies. I will find them and discipline them accordingly.*

But really, what politician wants to sound that dramatic about his or her staff? Besides, a truthful rewrite would probably look like this:

> *Sure I lied, but do you think I'm really going to admit it? So I'm going to stall until I can find someone else to blame.*

We'll talk more about the passive voice in the section on plain language. For now, think noun–verb, noun–verb.

Noun Nuggets: To Do and Not To Do

Nouns. We love them, but face it: they're weak. They don't have much energy and they rank low in terms of motivating the reader, unless of course you're using nouns such as "money," "prison," or the most motivating of all, "scandal." But for your routine business communications, the nouns must know their place and keep it. Here are some pointers:

◆ Stick to nouns that people actually say, and avoid the nouns people only say—or only *write*—at work. You know, when you write something like: "The project completion is due on Monday." What exactly is a "completion"? It puts readers off and sounds strange compared to: "We'll complete the project on Monday."

◆ Never write an all-noun subject line in an e-mail. Your subject line must have pizzazz, energy, spark...just to get the reader to open it. So make sure you complement the more standstill nouns with verbs that ignite the motion of the message.

For example, one of my clients sent regular e-mails to encourage employees and managers to nominate employees for awards. These awards, by the way, actually involve money, paid time off, and a desirable spot in the parking lot. So you'd think people would rush in with nominations—especially since they could even nominate themselves. But no. Nothing. One problem could be the noun-cluttered subject line:

Task 14567-002: Quarterly Directors Award.

Really exciting. Really fast. Right? The thing practically screams:

BORING. DON'T OPEN! LACKLUSTER NOUNS WITHIN!!

How much better if she wrote something like:

Nominate your coworker for something great!

Or:

Your chance to nominate! Don't miss out!

Or what one of my clients recommended:

And the winner is...

... and begin the actual e-mail with:

...that's your choice.

◆ Avoid starting your bullets with nouns. They sag, causing the entire sentence to droop with them. Besides, you end up starting each bullet with the same word—usually the topic of the sentence. In this example, I started the bullets with "stick to," "never write," and "avoid." I could have started this way:

Nouns that people actually say are fine, but avoid the ones you only use when writing.

Nouns make the motion of your e-mail subject line stand still, so who's going to open it?

Nouns cause your bullets to sag when you have them first in the sentence.

Boring, isn't it?

Noun Uppers

Naturally, we can't have a discussion about nouns without addressing which ones are uppercase. Most nouns aren't. The uppercase variety is reserved for the specific name of a person or thing—aka "formal nouns." Why they call them "formal" I'm not sure—they aren't especially formal, especially when you get into nicknames like "Biffy," "Bev," and "Bunny." But that's beside the point. Take a look at this example:

Forest Grove Junior High School was located in Worcester, Massachusetts.

The formal nouns are "Forest Grove Junior High School" and "Worcester, Massachusetts." This seems pretty straightforward, and naturally, you may feel like a dolt if you're not sure how to use them. Don't worry—it's not you. The whole matter can be quite confusing, especially since people can call themselves, their firms, pets, magazines, newspapers, even children, whatever they want— uppercase, lowercase, the choice is theirs.

For example, when speaking about our own U.S. government, would you say: "Federal," or "federal"? The answer: depends on the administration. Years ago, I was part of a White House initiative on plain language under Bill Clinton. Back then, within governmental documents, they capitalized it as "Federal." When Bush got elected, government writers everywhere held their breaths and waited. Uppercase "F" or lowercase "f"? Naturally rumors flew and arguments ensued until the new administration made the decision and the truth was revealed. I don't remember who revealed it, but the upper "F" stayed in official documents. And Washington heaved a collective sigh.

The plot thickens with names of newspapers or businesses. Remember, you can name your business anything you want. So you have bizarre names such as the engineering firm CH2M HILL. Why is the "CH2M" all uppercase? What does CH2M even mean? As for the "HILL," why is that uppercase? I called to find out, and got this response from a receptionist there: The CH2M stands for the initials of the founding engineers—Cornell, then Howland and Hays (that's the "2H"), and Merryfield. Later a company named "Hill" joined them, hence the "HILL." Well, sort of. When I asked the receptionist why the "HILL" was all uppercase, she informed me it wasn't. It's actually "Hill."

"But on your Website, it's 'HILL,'" I said.

"I know," she returned, "but it's really 'Hill.'"

"Then why is it 'HILL' on the site?"

"Don't know," she said. "Maybe it's marketing."

But as I said, it's their name. This odd name syndrome runs rampant. Years back when I was a journalist, I sent an article to the *Boston Globe*. Or was it *The Boston Globe*? When I called to find out, the receptionist said they use one for the morning edition and one for the evening edition. Which was which I can't remember. Then, there's the world famous magazine. You'll probably recognize the name, but which is correct?

◆ *The Atlantic Monthly*

◆ the *Atlantic* monthly

◆ the atlantic monthly

◆ the *Atlantic Monthly*

◆ *The Atlantic* monthly

I'm embarrassed to admit the answer is *The Atlantic* monthly. The magazine, *The Atlantic*, which appears once a month, has "monthly" on the cover. So lots of people, including yours truly, thought the "monthly" was part of the name. One of my teachers was an editor there, and for years I sent material, always addressing the envelope the wrong way. Fortunately, and uncharacteristically, he never mentioned it.

Then, you can't forget the defiant companies whose names are lowercase only. Or the ones whose Web address is part of their name. You may be thinking of Amazon.com. Or is that amazon.com? Or maybe Amazon.Com? The name on their Website is "amazon.com"—but that's their logo. The name they use in the text: Amazon.com. But how would you know that? The answer: you wouldn't. And all the usage rules won't help you. So how do you know what's right? Look on the Website or call.

Acronyms: The Naked Nouns

Surely you know acronyms. They're the abbreviations speckled through every government, professional, or industry document. What becomes an acronym and what doesn't depends on who's using it. Some people create names for their organization or program partly because it sounds great as an acronym.

Take Mothers Against Drunk Driving (MADD) and Students Against Drunk Driving (SADD). The group changed its name recently, without losing its acronym, and is now known as Students Against Destructive Decisions. Other names just orient themselves to acronyms such as LBJ or RFK, but you don't see GWB for President George W. Bush, although you did see a lot of "W"s during the election year. As for William Jefferson Clinton? No WJC—he was always "Bill."

How you determine the correct acronym for an organization, project, or anything else is same as how you determine the upper- and lowercase of a name: look at the Website or call. If they get the acronym wrong, then it's their fault. Here are some other acronym pointers:

◆ Write the name first, put the acronym in parenthesis, and then use the acronym in subsequent references. That is, unless the name IS an acronym, like CH2M Who-Ever-Else-They-Are Hill. Then you have a great defense when Grammar Mavens start clicking their tongues.

◆ Remind the reader what the acronym stands for if you're writing a two-or-more-page document. Your reader might forget what you said on page one once they reach page four. Even more likely, they'll jump from page to page or paragraph to paragraph, skimming as they go. Which means they may not see the written name.

◆ Skip the name altogether if the reader is more familiar with the acronym. CIA and FBI are two good examples. Which brings up another point. The decision about whether you only need the

acronym—and not the spelled-out noun—
depends on region, the reader's familiarity with
the name, and other factors.

If you live in Washington, D.C. for example, you immediately
know that GSA is the organization that oversees federal buildings.
But if you live just about anywhere else and don't work for the
government, "GSA" might sound like a health food store or a
clothing designer. This leads to the last acronym point.

◆ Tell the reader a little about the organization
the first time you mention it—assuming they
don't already know. So you'd say: "I'm dying to
work at the General Services Administration
(GSA), the agency that manages government-
owned property."

By the way, this concept applies to any name, whether it involves
an acronym or not. So for example, if you said: "I'm taking the
kids to the White House on Saturday," do you need to define
"White House"? Actually, yes, if you intended to take the kids to
the White House on Saturday for a burger and fries. To avoid
confusion, you'd say: "I'm taking the kids to the White House—
that burger joint on 2nd Street—on Saturday for a burger and
fries. You want to join me?"

A Quick Q&P Acronym Q&A

Who could believe so much can get tucked into a few little
letters? But in my years of training professional people, acronyms
have a sort of mystique about them. Not to mention, they're
annoying. How do you use them? When do you use them? What
if you have too many of them? So many questions. So little time.
But never fear, here are some answers.

Q. How about a glossary? Should our company have an
acronym glossary on our Website?
A. Plenty of people do—not just for acronyms but for
jargon and difficult industry terms too. Frankly, I'm
against them. These days you have to work hard
enough just to get your readers to read your message.

Even if you write material the readers allegedly *have* to read, you still have to ward off the possibility they'll skim. So a glossary? What are the odds they'll actually use it? And why make them work to catch your meaning? Especially since their attention span is so limited, and you want them focusing on reading and responding the right way—*not* on catching up on how your organization uses nouns. My advice: Skip the glossary and embed the full name, and any necessary descriptions, as you use the acronym.

Q. What if our most important readers know what the acronym means—should we write out the full name? I'm afraid we won't seem professional if we do.

A. Okay, a few more reading realities. To start, since many documents now appear on the Web for all to see, your language must be as transparent and inclusive as possible. Another reality: tasks have become so specialized, the intricacies of your job may be outrageously alien to the guy in the cubicle next to you. Then there's your customer, whether an internal person or the quintessential decision-maker who signs the check. Can you assume this person knows the acronym, even though his or her employees may know it? My advice: It's better to safely write out and define the acronym than lose your reader.

Q. But what if I'm only using the acronym once? Do I need to write out the full noun then?

A. No, you don't...need to use the acronym, that is. Just write out the name and skip the acronym since they won't need to know it. Unless, of course, they'll see the acronym in other communications your organization sends and you want consistency from one message to the next.

Q. What if we have the same acronym for two different things?

A. I've seen this happen before. It's pretty amazing. Suddenly employees realize they're having one conversation, using one acronym, but lo and behold, talking about two different things. If you encounter this situation, don't panic. Just rename one of your acronyms by adding another letter, or if your organization steadfastly wants the duplication, add some little clue. If your acronym is "ABC," then say "ABC-1" and "ABC-2."

Q&P Break: Tell All

Know any outrageous names or acronyms—good, bad, or simply stunning? Then send them in for possible posting. Just go to: *www.quickandpainlessbusinesswriting.com.*

More Noun Nuggets: The Secrets

The best-kept secret about empowering your nouns and creating a knock-out message lies in one word: specific. Be specific. Here's the short list of advantages:

◆ More information *without* more words.

◆ Better read for the restless reader.

◆ More exact impression so the readers can actually *see* what you're saying in their minds' eyes.

For example, read this sentence:

Last night, my friend was attacked by a dog.

What does the dog look like? What became of your poor friend? Is this situation traumatic? Dramatic? The plot thickens with a more specific noun:

Last night, my friend was attacked by a Doberman Pinscher.

Now you envision the hospital visit, intensive care, scars that last a lifetime. You can also touch up the noun "my friend," for more effect. If someone named Betsy Bloom got attacked, the consequences would be ever more tragic than if the victim was Mighty Mike Moran. But wait! The plot twist doesn't end there. Here's what really happened:

Last night, my friend Mike Moran was attacked by a toy poodle.

Now you imagine a toy poodle hanging off an enormously large pant leg.

General–Specific Cheat Sheet

General Word
Jose and I attended the *event.*
The *participants* were inspirational.
We received interesting *reading material.*

Specific I
Jose and I attended the *opera.*
Placido Domingo was inspirational.
We received an interesting *libretto.*

Specific II
Jose and I attended the *co-op.*
The *Revolutionary Front* was inspirational.
We received an interesting *proclamation sheet.*

Genderless-ness: Language Battles in Action

One of the more obvious—and controversial—language shifts concerns (no surprise) gender. As you probably know, we once had firemen, policemen, milkmen, and so on. As if every profession revolved around men (except perhaps nurse, teacher, and of course, mom).

Eventually, people noticed that some of the cops on the beat were wearing ponytails and couldn't grow a beard if they tried. They also noticed that plenty of executives, political leaders, scientists, and professors weren't men. They were women. But more than that, they were women who were talking about opportunity, and adding new words to our national dialogue, such as "glass ceiling."

So the discussion went something like this:

"How do you know the person you're talking about is a man?"

"We don't."

Then, the argument went: "The 'man' stands for *all* people, not just males."

The counter-argument: "Why should 'man' represent all people? Why not 'woman'? Or 'person'?"

The response: "Because, that's how it is and that's how it has always been. Why be so petty?"

Then, the response really got heated and went something like this: "We're petty—you're petty! Hey—we have babies, hold jobs, make money, spend money! Face it: We deserve our own nouns, too!"

Well let me tell you, the transition wasn't easy. Alternatives flew with plenty of eye gouging—metaphorical and otherwise. Was it "fireperson"? How about "Fire Professional"? Eventually, they settled on "firefighter," "mail carrier," and, you know the list.

Other words gravitated to the more neutral side of things. When was the last time you met a "poetess" or "authoress"? No, they fluttered away with the petticoat and now we have the "poet" and "author." Oh—and remember the writing rule you learned way back when? About being consistent? Well, now's a good time to forget it. Because we may not have poetesses but we do have "hostesses," even mega-millionaire hostesses like Martha Stewart, and "heiresses," such as Paris Hilton, who is also an "actress." Of sorts.

But Wait! There's More!

Think the saga ends there? How about that word "woman?" It's still *half* man, and women are not *half*-men; they're 100 percent women. How about the more genderless "womyn"? Okay, you may be rolling your eyes and scoffing. Don't scoff. That's what people did when "firefighter" came in.

Granted, "womyn" will probably never take hold. Even feminist writers don't want it to change and here's the reason: According to Miller and Swift's *Handbook of Nonsexist Writing* (Harper Perennial, 1988), in its original form, "man" meant a person, whether male or female. "Wer" meant man, and "wif" meant woman, making "waepman" an adult man and "wifman" an adult woman. So the idea that "woman" is nothing without the "man" is pure myth.

Genderless Action Plan

What's your best action plan when it comes to genderless writing? Use common sense and go with the most prevalent usage. If everyone says "flight attendant," why say "stewardess"? Besides, you'll have to call those male stewardesses "stewards" and everyone will think you're on a boat. Most of the genderless changes will flow from you naturally, but if you do need to make a decision, my advice is, go for the most genderless alternative. You won't offend anyone and everyone will know what you mean.

Genderless-ness: The Ms., Miss, and Mrs. Dilemma

This one is so hot, trust me, you'll be toast if you get near it. I know this firsthand. In the old days, we called women "Miss" or "Mrs." depending on their marital status. Every woman fell into one of those two categories, although we called men "Mr." and got additional information from their ring fingers. Then, things changed and "Ms." (pronounced "mizz") was born.

You may be thinking "bra-burning," "women's lib," and all that. Actually, no. According to Miller and Swift, as far back as the early 1940s, secretarial handbooks started listing "Ms." as a Miss/Mrs. alternative. *Then* came the 1960s when those bra-burners, women's libbers, and others with good-old-fashioned common sense adopted "Ms." Actually, they insisted on it. Why should women be identified by their marital status and not men? What difference did their marital status make anyway?

After considerable debate, the nation agreed to adopt "Ms.," although not entirely. Plenty of people still disagree; some vehemently. Years ago, I wrote an article about the subject that appeared in newspapers nationwide. My point: The "Miss" and

"Mrs." really bring little value and "Ms." will probably win the race.

Normally, when I publish opinion pieces about communications, I get mail. Sometimes I get fan letters from people who just *love* what I have to say. Other times I get hate mail—particularly long, rambling letters from authors, names omitted. But with this opinion piece? I got hate mail, all right...in handwritten notes on flowery cards from elderly women. How dare I undermine the establishment of marriage? They were married for 50 years! They deserve the "Mrs." before their name! How dare I try to take it away?

The debate didn't end there. Shortly after, I was a guest on an NPR (National Public Radio) station about a book I had written on the writing process—one of those call-in talk shows that last a good hour. In the opening interview, I happened to mention—and I mean *mention*—that "Ms." is fast replacing "Mrs." in the workplace.

Then the calls came. And came. And came...all of them about "Ms.": some vehemently in favor, some against. No mere feminist issue, this concerned the evolution of the species and language as we know it. My host was delighted—what radio show doesn't embrace hard-core debate? The callers were hot. As for me? I was stunned into uncharacteristic silence. It's just two letters. Use it—but no one's recommending the death penalty if you don't.

Today "Ms." still stands strong, although "Mrs." and "Miss" still stand right there with it. So here's what you do:

◆ If a woman identifies herself as "Miss," "Mrs.," or "Ms.," call her that regardless of your own tastes, or even the norm in your organization.

◆ If you don't know what the woman calls herself, avoid the issue altogether by using her full name—no "Miss," "Mrs.," or "Ms." As in: "Dear Shirley Newhouse." Plenty of people do it and the practice is only growing as the world shrinks, names change, and you have no idea whether the reader is a man or a woman, let alone married.

◆ If your boss insists that you use *something*, use "Ms." I'm not saying that to win the NPR debate or make the elderly readers feel bad. It's a safe route in uncertain times.

◆ What if your boss insists that you use *something*—but definitely not "Ms."? Some consider using "Miss/Mrs." So yes, consider it. Briefly. Then use "Miss."

A Revealing "Ms." Alternative That No One Ever Considered and Never Took Hold

According to Miller and Swift, you should use "Mrs." for married *or* single *women*. That's what they did in the 17th and 18th centuries. *Girls*, meanwhile, were called "Miss," as in "mistress." Of course, "mistress" had a second meaning: a concubine or prostitute.

Chapter 3
Noun Accomplices:
Articles, Pronouns, and Adjectives

Articles

Articles are everywhere but few in number: just "the," "a," and "an." They're *so* quick and easy to use, almost everyone's an expert. Still, some questions do arise, so here's a quick article Q&A.

Another Quick Q&P Q&A...This Time About Articles

Q. When do you use "a" and when do you use "the"?

A. Use "a" aka the "indefinite" article when you mean a person or thing in general. For example, after dinner someone might say: "I am dying for a piece of cake." They don't mean a specific cake—any cake will do. But inside a bakery, you'd say: "I want the delicious-looking yellow cake—*the* one right there, on the left. Nope, not *the* one in *the* middle. *The* one on *the* left." In English teacher circles, "the" is known as the "definite" article.

Q. How about "a" and "an"? When should I use these articles?

A. Use "a" before a consonant (as I just did) and "an" before a vowel. Here are some examples:

A collection of coins was missing from the office.

An article appeared in the newspaper about it.

Later, a housekeeper found the coins behind a desk somewhere.

The letter "h" takes "a" or "an" depending on whether the "h" has a hard or soft pronunciation. See the difference:

A good housekeeper must be an honest person.

Q. What if I'm writing about a country? There's only one of them, so shouldn't I write "the" first? Like "The France."

A. Actually, no and yes. You don't need an article before formal names in general, so for example you wouldn't say: "The General McArthur," right? Sure, you would say: "The general, the one who was holding a drink at the Christmas party," but that's because you didn't use that person's actual name. Similarly, you wouldn't say: "The France has great food," or "The Spain has beautiful mountains." Before you get too secure in this rule, remember that you *would* say, "*The* Netherlands has cold winters," and "*The* United States has a formidable presence around the world." But those are exceptions.

Q. What if I have a list? Should I repeat the article?
A. That question deserves a more intricate answer than you might think. The short version: "It depends." The long version: "It depends on the rhythm you want for your sentence." For example, you can write:

Remember to bring the uniforms, shin guards, flip charts, and markers so we can remind the players of the rules of the game.

But if you want to emphasize just how many things your assistant must carry, add articles. They prolong the sentence and emphasize every new noun:

Remember to bring the uniforms, the shin guards, the flip charts, and the markers so we can remind the players of the rules of the game.

Here, notice how the articles in this line play up our fictional friend Ethel's many demands:

Ethel wanted a salary increase, a new office, a few extra weeks vacation, and a personal assistant, or she'd quit.

Then, observe how in this sentence the absent articles help downplay the items in the list...and play up "personal assistant":

Valerie agreed to Ethel's salary increase, new office, and extra vacation weeks, but not the personal assistant.

Where to Go for More

If you need further rule advice about articles or anything else, try Purdue University's Online Writing Lab at *owl.english.purdue.edu*. They even have exercises and plenty of examples, for when you're in doubt.

The Article Cheat Sheet

The

The apple on the table looks delicious.

I live under *the bridge* on South E Street.

The file contains *the missing* information.

The director never takes vacations.

A/An

I am dying to eat *an apple*.

If you live under *a bridge*, your walls will shake.

All papers should go in *a file*.

A director needs *a vacation* now and then.

Pronouns: The Rule Breakers

You know pronouns: the seemingly harmless little words such as "he," "she," "they," and "ours." If nouns are the alphas in the sentence, pronouns are the servants, busily doing the dirty work. They follow the noun, replacing it so the sentence isn't endlessly boring and confusing. So rather than say: "Carl sure looks bulked up since Carl started working out at MM&M Gym," you say: "Carl sure looks bulked up since *he* started working out at MM&M Gym."

And really, when considering pronouns, how complicated can you get? Basically, just make sure the reader knows who the pronoun refers to. Look at this sentence: "Harry spied Carl leaving MM&M Gym. Boy, he looked tired." Obviously, "he" refers to "Carl." For one thing, Carl is closer to the pronoun "he" than "Harry," so logic dictates "he" must refer to "Carl."

What could be easier, right? Only, a few other matters sally forth, causing pronoun problems. Here are the big ones:

I-phobia

Most certainly you remember the old high school rule to limit how many times you use "I"—or avoid it altogether. Using the

"I," it seems, indicated you were narcissistic and at great risk of boring the reader with your love of self. So you probably developed an I-phobia. Then rather than say:

I tested the fruit flies' reproductive capabilities for five years, over which time I scrupulously recorded the findings.

You suck the "I" right out of the sentence and say:

The fruit flies' reproductive capabilities were tested for five years over which time the findings were scrupulously recorded.

What happened to the alpha noun—or in this case pronoun? Who is doing the action? No one knows but the fruit fly. This "I"-avoidance theme only heightened when you entered college and your academic advisors told you *not* to use the "I" at *all*, ever. It also becomes a problem when you consider the dreaded passive voice, which we'll discuss in Chapter 8.

Why, you wonder, should the "I" be banished? Are academics, researchers, and high school students such despicable people they dare not mention themselves in the same breath as, say, fruit flies? I guess that depends on the person. But the reasoning was more along the lines of "You want the reader to focus on the subject, not the person discussing the subject." Oddly, researchers *can* speak of themselves in the third person. As in:

The researcher carefully scrutinized the reproductive organs of the fruit fly. The fruit fly appeared unscathed and happily flew away.

Anyway, don't worry about the "I." It's there for a reason. You should worry about repeating points and being wordy and that type of thing, but the "I" is okay. I think so. I really do.

Me-phobia

True or false:

- *Toby and me collected fruit flies.*
- *I bought the pastry for Dana and me.*

◆ *While at Mike's Mass and Muscle Gym, Henry and me spotted unsightly fruit flies.*

Probably you know that numbers one and three are incorrect. But did you know that number two *is* correct? If so, congratulations, you won't make that mistake and can move on. If not, congratulations, you have something to learn and got more bang for your buck from this book than the other guy.

Plenty of people, so accustomed to their teachers, parents, and grandparents correcting them every time they said things such as: "Pete and me are going to collect fruit flies down at the gym" developed a phobia and dropped the "me" altogether. So they end up saying: "Hands off! That jar of fruit flies belongs to Pete and I."

You may already know the secret to determining I/me correctness. If not, here's what you do: Cover the noun that comes before the "I" or "me." If the sentence sounds right, it is. If not, change the pronoun from "I" to "me" or vice versa. It works this way:

The sentence: *Toby and me collected fruit flies.*
The cover-up: —— *me collected fruit flies.*
The decision: Does the sentence sound right? No, it doesn't.
The revision: *Toby and I collected fruit flies.*

Or you could have a sentence like this:
The sentence: *The fruit fly eggs equally belong to Toby and I.*
The cover-up: *The fruit fly eggs equally belong to* —— *I.*
The decision: That sentence doesn't sound right either.
The revision: *The fruit fly eggs equally belong to Toby and me.*

By the way, when writing about yourself and someone else, you should list the other person first and yourself last, as in "Come catch flies with Toby and me," instead of "with me and Toby." I don't know why, but trust me—it's not personal.

Of course, this is much harder when you're *speaking* about Toby, the fruit flies, and yourself and you can't really slow down to do the calculation. Thankfully, the mistake will be less obvious, too.

The Myself and I Syndrome

This one's easy. If you make this mistake, don't sweat it too much. Everyone will know what you mean and probably no one except the Grammar Mavens will notice. Look at this example of what *not* to do and see if you can guess what's wrong and why:

As for myself, I enjoy a good bowl of chili for breakfast.

Find the problem? "Myself" is like a mirror, reflecting the "me" or the "I," which means the "myself" should come second in the sentence. So you should write:

I, myself, enjoy a good bowl of chili for breakfast.

Or you could get out of the whole problem and say:

As for me, I enjoy a good bowl of chili in the morning.

Your (a) Gold Star

Even higher on the list of the Grammar Mavens' banes is using "your" when you mean "you're," and vice versa. Plenty of people make the mistake of confusing the two. If you ask me, the confusion isn't a carnal sin…but not everyone agrees with me. At the very least, the mistake can distract from your meaning. So here's the difference: "Your" means you own something, as in: "Is this *your* bowl of chili?" Use this one when you need to indicate possession of something. "You're," on the other hand, is the contraction of "you are," as in: "You're a chili lover." In case you're concerned you might be guilty of this offense, every time you write "you're," say it without the contraction. As in: "After the meeting, Tom asked if this was you're bill." You are bill? Nope—doesn't work. It's *your* bill.

The Its-It's Conundrum

"It" takes varied forms. You have "it"—as a genderless pronoun for items that have no gender, such as rocks. So you'd say: "Wow! Pete will never be able to lift that rock! *It* must weigh at least 100 pounds." And naturally you'd say: "Then what is Pete supposed to do? It's blocking his driveway." Now, the "it's" means "it is" and the sentence works to perfection.

The confusion lies in "its." As in: his, hers, its, theirs. Called the possessive pronoun, this baby needs no apostrophe, but people forget and write: "It's sides are rough as barbed wire—he'll definitely need gloves." What they're really saying is "It *is* sides are rough as barbed wire..." which makes no sense at all, and should be "Its sides..."

If you think you're making this mistake, say the whole thing, "it is," every time you write "it's" until you get it right consistently.

But wait—the pronoun saga doesn't end here. You see, our harmless little pronouns lead secret lives, defiant lives, breaking rules and causing general havoc. It all started years ago, when we referred to people in general as "he." I don't mean androgyny types—I mean general or hypothetical ones. For example:

When a person is working out, he should try not to groan too loudly.

This was around the time when "firemen" became "firefighters." The argument was similar to the one about genderless nouns, and went something like this:

The argument: Everyone knows that we mean men and women when we use 'he.' What difference does it make?"

The counter-argument: "If it doesn't make any difference, why don't we use 'she' instead?"

"Because we already use 'he.' Why confuse things?"

"*We're* not confusing things, you are. How can anyone know if you mean an actual 'he' or a 'he-and-she' he?"

"They can tell by the sentence. Besides using 'he' is the rule."

"Well, we should change that rule. You *can* change rules, you know. It's not like they're scientific formulas. Like we don't call policemen 'policemen' anymore, we call them 'officers,' or if you're in a bad mood, 'cops.'"

...and so on.

Eventually, the impossibility of using "he" for both genders became clear to almost everyone. But what to use instead? That's when the havoc started. Writers' groups discussed it, linguists debated it, and editors did whatever they wanted. In the end, the options boil down to these:

Option 1: He or she. Some people dislike this option because they feel like they're adding extra words. But not if you consider "he or she" as one word, sort of like "myself" is one word (combining "my" with "self"). Only with "he or she," leave in the spaces.

Option 2: She/he or he/she. You still see this one in form letters but it has left the scene in professional letters, reports, and almost every other document. The reason: When people read, they usually pronounce what they see—if not actually move their lips. So how do you say 'he/she'? Heeshee? The combination is awkward and makes you sound more like a machine than a live person. Besides, as one of my clients pointed out, if you add "it" to the list, to include the genderless set, you're left with "she/he/it." Now, go ahead, say it.

My advice: avoid "she/he" completely.

Option 3: They. I like this one—it sounds the most natural. I'm sure you've said or heard something like this: "When a person is hungry, they should reach for the nearest bowl of chili." However, many people object to this option because they think it's inconsistent: You can't really have *a* single person and use *they*, which designates more than one person. But it's not much different than the perfectly acceptable "you" that can refer to one person or 100 people. If "you" can do it, why can't "they"? And remember, the English language is consistently inconsistent.

Option 4: He...she. Reserve this one for long documents like 20-page instructions, lengthy newsletters, or books if you happen to write one. The idea is that you use "he" for five or so pages then switch to "she" for five or so pages, giving equal time for both. Personally, I find this option irritating, but that's just me.

Option 5: Use the noun or a substitute noun again. This option can sound boring and was probably the reason for pronouns in the first place: "When the manager calls, tell the manager to meet me at 10:00," or "When the manager calls, tell this person to meet me at 10:00."

Option 6: One. I added this option in the interest of full disclosure, *not* because I think it's a good idea. But some people, for their own reasons, like to use it. So you might say: "If one so desires, one can chose to forsake the conference and attend to the beach instead." Sadly, "one" is overly formal, in a day when a more relaxed business tone is a must, and lends itself to antiquated words like "forsake" and "attend to." If you're aspiring to have a British butler, or become one yourself, use it. Otherwise, find something else.

Pronoun Cheat Sheet

Pronoun	Example
I	I enjoy chili.
you	You enjoy chili.
he or she	He or she enjoys chili.
we	We enjoy chili.
they	They enjoy chili.

And Ever More Pronouns...

Do you remember possessive pronouns? We mentioned them when discussing the "it's/ its" distinction. They indicate you that you own—or possess—something. As in the "my" in this sentence:

Have you seen my man?

And the "hers" here:

We thought that guy was hers.

And the "our" here:

Actually, it's none of our business.

There's nothing especially new to discuss about these pronouns—just make sure you're clear about which noun the pronoun stands in for. And in case you're a little foggy, or just want a reminder, use this cheat sheet.

Possessive Pronoun Cheat Sheet

Pronoun	Sentence
my	Do you know who took my shoes?
your	Is this your hat?
his, hers, its	This is *his* cat, not hers.
	Do you know where its mouse went?
our	Our favorite jokes involve penguins.
your	Is this your best effort?
their	Their clothes tended to be green.

The Great Who/Whom Debate

We discussed this already—but let's delve. "Whom" has just about left spoken language for almost everyone under 80 years old (Grammar Mavens excepted) and promises to leave written language soon, although not soon enough. Then you won't have to suffer through stodgy sentences such as:

To whom does that gold lamé dress belong?

Soon we can find safe shelter with sentences such as:

Who does that gold lamé dress belong to?

My advice: forget the "whom." Trust me, no one will miss it.

Adjectives

Adjectives, those quick, clean words usually wedged before or after nouns, endure as a favorite of kids everywhere. They can write a story about an unremarkable patch of woods in their backyard and turn it into:

A dark, damp forest with shuddering leaves and ghostly shadows.

And imagine the possibilities for love:

How I loved his dark, luminous eyes and his lips full and red as juicy, ripe cherries.

61

In the 1800s, authors used endless adjectives, talking about heaving bosoms; wringing hands; great, thunderous sobs; those kinds of things. These days, the reader wants *quick*, sassy messages. Immediate information. Tight words. So adhere to this adjective adage: Never use five adjectives where one will do.

Maintain necessary information. If you're describing a landscape that's mountainous, dry, windswept, *and* expansive—better pick and chose. What matters most? Dry? Expansive? All are important, you say? Then keep them, but prepare the reader for what's ahead with something like: "The landscape had three features…" Even better, throw in a little teaser adjective like: "The landscape had three amazing or remarkable or unexpected or unusual features…" to prime the reader for what's ahead.

Beware of duplication. Don't repeat the description using different words. "The high mountain which is a towering 500 feet" is redundant. Which adjective should you use? As Miss Ferguson might have said, "What do you think?"

Put the most important adjective first. Actually, put the most important *anything* first—word, point, or description. The first in line wins the most attention from the reader and stands a higher chance of being remembered.

Use specifics. Specifics let the readers see for themselves. The mountain is high? Who says? Why should they believe you? It's possible they don't even know you. And even if they should believe you, because, say, you're an expert in mountain terrain, they're more likely to be believe you if they can see that mountain for themselves. This leads to another matter. How high is high? A 12-foot mountain may be enormously high if you live in Kansas. The statement is simply too subjective for the reader to believe—they need some type of evidence so they can see for themselves.

Advertisers know this principle well, by the way. They don't say: "An enormously big sale!" because how big is "enormously big"? Especially when it comes to money? So they say "Up to 50 percent off all Home Decorating Items." You've got to give them credit, too. They say "up to" so they don't have to use real descriptors such as: "3–5 percent off *some* home decorating items, and a few that no one wants are 50 percent off, but the rest cost 100 percent the same price."

Anyway, back to mountains. Notice the difference in these specifics:

- ◆ Specific #1: "The mountain is 25 feet high," gets an "oh" from the reader.

- ◆ Specific #2: "The mountain is 50 feet high," gets a "wow" from the reader.

- ◆ Specific #3: "The mountain is 500 feet high," gets a "you're kidding!" from the reader. *Especially* if the mountain is in Kansas.

A final case for using specific adjectives: general ones sound boring. I know, you may be thinking you're not in the business of entertaining your reader; you're just trying to get them to do something. But entertainment value never hurts. Let's return to that mountain one last time. How many times have you used the word high? As in:

Boy, the prices of gas these days sure are high.

Our hotel room was pretty high up—you should have seen the view.

After the conference I had a few drinks on an empty stomach—boy was I high.

You get the picture, right? But how many times do you hear specifics such as "500 feet"? Even the novelty of the word (or in this case, the number) should help. Of course, those specifics don't have to be quantifiable. Say you're marketing ice cream. You could say:

Jumpin' Joe's new Caramel Ice Cream is good.

The flat and uninspired "good," secretly signals to the reader: "Jumpin' Joe's New Caramel Ice Cream tastes about as good as cardboard, only sweeter." But use a real standout adjective and imagine the possibilities:

Jumpin' Joe's new Caramel Ice Cream is sumptuous.

Jumpin' Joe's new Caramel Ice Cream is positively decadent.

Or you could go way out like Campbell's Soup and make your own adjective such as "Mm-mm good."

General/Specific Adjective Cheat Sheet

Could be anything adjectives
Trish has interesting lips.
Coffee Cap Café has an unusual selection of coffees.
Don drives an unusual MG.

Could be good adjectives
Trish has soft, supple lips.
Coffee Cap Café has South American and Asian coffees.
Don drives a glittery, gold MG.

Could be bad adjectives
Trish has cracked, dry lips.
Coffee Cap Café has bitter coffees of dubious origins.
Don drives a rusted 1979 MG.

Q&P Break: The Sweep

You'd be amazed at how few people use specifics when describing things. But it really helps, especially when you're supporting a point such as why a prospective client should choose your firm and not someone else's. Writing a recommendation or self evaluation? Those specific adjectives are imperative. You haven't been in the field for a long time. You've been in the field for 10 years. So go ahead, pull out one of those adjective-rich documents and check. Find general adjectives? Rewrite.

Chapter 4
Verbs:
The Power Words

No question, verbs reign as the mass and muscle of the word-use kingdom. They're strong. They're powerful. And boy do they stand out in a crowd! Why? Because verbs are about *energy*. 100 percent energy.

Let's do a quick noun–verb comparison. Say someone went into the room of Dolores, the bearded lady in the traveling circus. Naturally, you want to know who. No surprise: It's Bill the Sword Swallower, aka The Amazing Bill. All of this is interesting, but more interesting: what was Bill *doing* in Dolores's room? That's where the verb—also known in classrooms everywhere as the "predicate"—comes in. As always, specifics tell all. The more specific the verb, the better. Here's the sentence with a general verb:

Bill was in Dolores's room.

Here's a look at the specific possibilities behind this potentially seedy story:

◆ *Bill retrieved something from Dolores's room.*

◆ *Bill ransacked Dolores's room.*

◆ *Bill searched Dolores's room.*

◆ *Bill caroused in Dolores's room.* (With whom? Now the *noun* takes on new importance! But *not* without the verb.)

Your Reader's Energy Threshold

No threshold. The more exciting, energetic, revealing, and exact the verb, the more your reader will love it. Think of your verbs as a flavor. Go for spicy, tart, and poignant, and steer clear of vanilla!

Action Verbs

In the verb community, you'll find "action verbs" and "linking verbs." Say yes to action verbs and no to linking verbs, whenever possible. Let's start with action verbs. They express action, any action, whether a small event:

Martha threw her pencil...

or a major event:

Martha threw her pencil and it stuck in Gilbert's eye.

Of course, sometimes that event occurs inside your head, such as:

Gilbert instantly saw flashes of light and thoughts careened through his head...

or even inside your soul:

Martha withered in shame and horror.

Harnessing Verb Power:
A Quick and Painless Approach

As with nouns and adjectives, the more specific the verb, the more powerful the message. And writing is all about power. Sure "Ronny *left* the meeting." But by saying: "Ronny snuck out of the meeting," you add a new dimension of possibility and intrigue. Here are some other examples:

Wimpy: *We* wanted *Derek to* tell *us the truth.*

Strong: *We* insisted *Derek* reveal *the truth.*

Analysis: In the wimpy example, Derek could be hiding anything: information about who let the coffee burn in the office snack room or the real price of the holiday party door prize. In the strong example, Derek holds a potentially valuable secret.

Wimpy: *I* go *to Cambry's every Friday.*

Strong: *I* rush *to Cambry's every Friday.*

Analysis: In the strong example, you know the author hurries to get there. Desperate for a drink? Off to meet that certain someone? Or simply anxious to get away from work?

You can refer to verbs such as "say," "ask," and "want" as "placeholder verbs." They simply hold, or occupy, a place in the sentence. Avoid placeholder verbs and favor more energetic options. For example, take this sentence:

Bill wants the job.

Big deal, right? Now, how about:

Bill aches for the job.

Or:

Bill is chasing the job.

Or even:

Bill could kill for that job.

The difference is in the degree. Besides, placeholders are boring to read—so liven it up a little to something more active. Here's another example:

Placeholder: *Felix said that Mandy is an egghead.*

Verb alternative: *Felix screamed that Mandy is an egghead.*

Verb alternative: *Felix whispered that Mandy is an egghead.*

How About Those Tense—and Slow and Painful—Verbs?

Unlike nouns, which basically remain the same, aside from the plurals and possessives we talked about earlier, verbs are shifty little creatures adapting new forms depending on circumstance. Or maybe they suffer from ADHD and simply cannot focus on the rules long enough to uphold them.

What other way to explain the seemingly endless deviations to tense? Sure, Melvin "steals" ideas from you all the time. But did Melvin "stealed" the idea he discussed at the meeting, as you might expect? No, he "stole" it. And sure, you might "speak" to Esther Carmichael, your boss, about this problem, but did you already "speaked" to her several times before...to no avail? No, of course not. You "spoke" to her.

So how do you address the endless tense deviations? Here are some pointers:

Q&P Break: Tense Pointers

Pointer #1: Don't agonize over it. I mean it. Not grasping all the intricacies about tense and person is *not* a personality deficit, an indication you're not smart, or most especially, a sign you have zero writing potential. It's possible you're an excellent writer. You just need to tame the wild exceptions until you're in control.

Pointer #2: Read. Read. Read. You'll pick up the nuances of tense that way. As I wrote earlier, it doesn't matter what you read—go ahead, pull that trashy novel off the library shelf and read away. Like the tabloids? Hey—no one can get enough Elvis! Only keep on reading. Late at night, on the subway as you commute to work, doesn't matter. Eventually, you'll absorb the right writing style and your tense problems will melt away.

Pointer #3: Remember that writing partner I mentioned in the introduction? If your writing partner spots an unsightly tense mistake—and trust me, we *all* make them—take notes. Then each time after you write, check for that problem, correct that problem, and check again. After a few days of doing this, you'll find that it melted away.

The Good Guy Verbs—A Reminder

Now here's the good news: Even though there are buckets of exceptions, plenty of verbs follow the rules. Nice, predictable, good guy verbs. You learned about these way back in grammar school. Here's a quick refresher, then we'll move on.

Past: No kidding, it happened in the past. All you have to add is "-ed," except for those gazillion exceptions. But why belabor *that* point? Here are some examples:

Jack lived *on an island.*

Each morning, the sunlight reflected *off the water in his bathroom mirror.*

He rowed *to his office each morning: a high-rise across the bay.*

We liked *to visit him. His butler* served *Vodka Collins for breakfast each morning.*

Present: Obvious. The here-and-now. Here goes:

Jack lives *in a modest apartment near the courthouse.*

Each morning, Jack consults *with his legal team about a matter concerning embezzlement.*

He walks *to their office two blocks down the street.*

His butler now works *for the CEO of the Howie-Howie hotel chain.*

Future: The future tense proves that English does have a philosophical edge. Basically, the future is the present with a little "will." Or to be more precise, it's the infinitive form ("to"-plus-verb) with "will" before it. Here's what I mean:

Jack swears he will beat those charges. (to beat)

He says the jury will see that his sneaky employees hid the information from him. (to see)

The public will understand that this was 'unintentional' embezzlement. (to understand)

If he pulls this off, we will see lots of cases involving 'unintentional' embezzlement in the future. (to see)

Instead of "will," you can also use "am," "is," or "are" with "going" before the infinitive:

After the trial, Jack is going to host a knock-out party. (to host)

I am going to show up at that party, no matter what! (to show up)

That's that for the ease of the past, present, and future. Now let's look at the simple, perfect, and continuous tenses. The words alone can give you heartburn, but what they really *mean* is pretty simple.

Simple: And speaking of simple...frankly, I have no idea why they call this the "simple" tense. It's not simple. How can a tense be simple? Oh well—just another case in which the words may not match the meaning, but no one knows why.

With the simple tense, you're talking about permanent or ongoing situations, so you might say:

Betsy works *for Dr. Connor.*

Betsy sits *at a desk directly in front of Dr. Connor's door and* guards *it like a pit bull.*

Betsy stops *anyone from* entering *without her permission.*

Everyone lives *in fear and dread of Betsy.*

Remember E

Usually, you should add a naked "s" to the end of your verbs, in cases like "Betsy works..." But sometimes you need to dress the "s" a little and add an "e" in cases like:

Occasionally Betsy dozes at her desk. Carlton watches her closely.

If you're talking about the past, naturally you'd add the "-ed" ending and say, for example: "Last week, we *waited* until Betsy went to the bathroom, then *rushed* into Dr. Connor's office."

Perfect: Perfect? Don't think so. Here's what it really is: When you're discussing some indefinable point in time, you add "has," "have," or "had" to the verb, as in…

Our team has *traveled to many countries to collect aquatic specimens.*

Ed has *worked hard to separate the algae from the amoebas.*

We had *used Jack's abandoned island retreat as home base.*

As for the future perfect: that's when an action will occur *before* something else in the future, as in:

We will have *cleared out our microscopes and dissecting equipment before Jack arrives home.*

Continuous: Remarkably, the continuous tense really *does* resemble its name: You use it when something continues to happen over a long or longish period of time. Just put "am," "is," "was," "were," "are," or "will be" before the verb and the "-ing" ending. So you'd say:

> *While in the field, Ed* was searching *for unusual specimens. The analysts* are examining *an unusual specimen Ed discovered. We* were considering *naming it 'Jack.'*

Use the past continuous when two things happened simultaneously:

> *Ed* was slipping *out the back door, while Jack, with two unknown accomplices,* was unloading *his new paper shredder.*

And—the future continuous?

> *I think Jack* will be enjoying *his freedom.*

Tense About Tense?

Memorizing the names of the tenses won't help a lot, but using them to your advantage will. A lot of people out there might tell you to keep it simple—in more ways than one. For example, they advise you to say:

> *Todd works in Dr. Fennel's office. Todd organizes the patient files. He also contacts patients about their medical diagnoses.*

So you see—we have the simple tense: very here, now, and always. We also have simple sentences: short and concise. Yes, everything simple, simple, simple. And annoying as a rash. To clear up the problem, play around with tense. Perhaps write:

> *In Dr. Fennel's office, Todd* has been organizing *the patient files and contacting patients about their medical diagnoses.*

Or you could say:

> *While working in Dr. Fennel's office, Todd organized patient files and contacted them about their medical diagnoses.*

This opens up the possibility of tension-building sentences, such as:

> *While working in Dr. Fennel's office, Todd organized patient files. He also contacted patients about their medical diagnoses, which is how the whole incident began.*

The Noun–Verb Marriage: A Brief Interlude

We discussed the noun–verb relationship earlier. Well, all verbs are not created equal in the eyes of the nouns that interact with them, which leads us to the transitive verb. The transitive verb isn't a problem for most people, but let's review it anyway.

In this sentence: "Todd organized..." he had to organize *something*, right? The verb transitions you to *what* he organized: the file. Remember, verbs aren't monogamous. So make sure you adequately attach them to the right nouns, whether one, two, or three of them. This sentence is rather lonely:

When organizing the files, Todd confused Ted Patterson's file...

But this sentence is not:

When organizing the files, Todd confused Ted Patterson's file with Trish Hartley's.

More about Todd, Ted, and Trish in Chapter 8. For now, one more transitive verb example:

Lonely verb—one noun only: *The turtle chased...*

Happy verb: *The turtle chased the frog...*

Really happy verb: *The turtle chased the frog across the lake.*

Remember! Action Happens!

Remember, sometimes action happens. No one and nothing receives it. Here are some examples:

The lettuce wilted.

The barbell glistened.

The tomato ripened.

The presentation bombed.

Tense Agreement: A Quick and Painless Approach

As with any good union, nouns and verbs must agree on how the whole arrangement works. So if a noun is singular, the verb must suit that singular fashion:

Billy Junior strokes the lion's mane.

If plural, you say:

The Becker twins stroke the lion's mane.

You probably do this instinctively. But sometimes you get into trouble with plural-ish words like "children." Singular? You have one clump of children, so maybe, but in that clump, you have 10, 15 kids...lots of them. So it's better to say: "The children *are* happy playing with the lion." The verb world is loaded with questionable and confusing combinations. Take a look:

Agreement Cheat Sheet

First person—one
I
No "s" on verb: I sign.

First person—more than one
we
No "s" on verb: John and I sign. We sign.

Second person—one or many
you
No "s" on verb: You sign.

Third person—one
he or she
Add "s" on verb: He signs and she signs.

Third person—more than one
they
No "s" on verb: They sign.

The Top 10 Agreement Hang-Ups

Is They Yours?

1. The hang-up: If I have a measurement such as a percent, fraction, part, whatever, I can't decide whether the verb should be plural or singular. This is embarrassing because I'm in finance.

Is this your hang-up? Take the test and see:

A. Two quarts of milk are missing.
B. Two quarts of milk is missing.
C. Both work; don't worry about it.
D. 25 percent of the company has the flu.
E. 25 percent of the company have the flu.
F. No one's got the flu, so don't worry about that, either.

Here's the answer: With measurements, the verb refers to the noun—and not the amount—involved. To be sure, knock off the amount, and you have: "The milk is missing..." and "The company has the flu." So the answer: B and D.

2. The hang-up: How about money and time? That's also big in my business. I'm never sure whether to make the verb singular or plural. I mean, if I have six dollars, that's lots of one dollar bills, right? So wouldn't the verb be plural?

Is this your hang-up? Take the test and see:

A. Six dollars are a lot to pay for milk.
B. Six dollars is a lot to pay for milk.
C. Avoid it and say: The milk costs a lot: six dollars.

Here's the answer: If you answered B, you're right. Always use the singular with time and money. But if you answered C, or *thought* you should answer C, but didn't because the rules didn't indicate two answers are allowed, you're doubly right. You should avoid the "to be" form "is" and use more interesting, and energetic alternatives. But that's for later in this chapter.

3. The hang-up: Say I'm using "who" to describe someone, then talk about them, as in "Derek is one of the employees who..." I get stuck. Should the verb be singular or plural?

Is this your hang-up? Take the test and see:

A. Derek is one of the Vice Presidents who is allegedly involved in a crime.

B. Derek is one of the Vice Presidents who are allegedly involved in the crime.

C. The Johnson Brothers is the team who investigate corporate crimes.

D. The Johnson Brothers are the team who investigates corporate crimes.

E. The Johnson Brothers is the team who investigates corporate crimes.

Here's the answer: Basically, do this: consider the noun just before the "who"—or "that" and "which" for that matter—to be the subject of the sentence and act accordingly. So "B" would be correct. As for the Johnson Brothers example—I know, I crammed a lot in there. The correct answer is "E": Consider the subject "the team" and add "investigates." As for the "Johnson Brothers is..." part, that's not part of this hang-up, but it's a warm-up for the next.

4. The hang-up: Okay, so I have no idea what to do when I have, what do you call it? A collective noun. You know, when the noun, such as "team," "staff," "group," or "corporate gang" has lots of nouns in it.

Is this your hang-up? Take the test:

A. The team pursues the truth with diligence and force.

B. The team pursue the truth with diligence and force.

C. The team is in disagreement about the second accomplice, but agree the first one was Jack.

D. The team are in disagreement about the second accomplice, but agree the first one was Jack.

E. All of the above.

Here's the answer: All of the above. Sort of. The correct answer depends on the situation. If the team acts as a unified whole, then "A" is correct. But if it acts as a bunch of separate entities bouncing off of each other, say in disagreement, that makes "C" correct. Only—and this is the "sort of" part—some guides disagree, like my grammar checker who insists on "is" and "pursues." So you decide. Remember that a strict, prescriptive approach to your business writing can only go so far (and grammar-checker programs aren't always right), so you should feel free to make the choice that sounds the best and most natural.

5. The hang-up: How about "each," "everyone," "every one," "everybody," "anyone," "anybody," "someone", and "somebody" as pronouns? When I use these, I get totally confused, you know, like when I'm saying: "Hmm, each of those muffins look delicious." Or is it: "Each of those muffins looks delicious"?

Is this your hang-up? Take the test:
A. Each of the investors thinks Derek did it.
B. Each of the investors think Derek did it.
C. Every one of Derek's neighbors knows he snuck out before the sentencing.
D. Every one of Derek's neighbors know he snuck out before the sentencing.

Here's the answer: Easy: It's A and C. Just consider these pronouns singular—no matter what comes after them. Oh, about that muffin: It would be: "Each of those muffins looks delicious."

6. The hang-up: I'm never sure what to do with the verb when I'm writing about two singular nouns using "or" or "nor" to connect them. I hate to give away anything in your next hang-up test, but what if I'm saying Jack or his butler did something like help Derek?

Is this your hang-up? Take the test:
A. Either Derek's business partner Jack or the accomplice is driving him to the dock.
B. Either Derek's business partner Jack or the accomplice are driving him to the dock.
C. Neither the judge nor the prosecutor know he will live comfortably on the island.
D. Neither the judge nor the prosecutor knows he will live comfortably on the island.

Here's the answer: You have two separate entities. You have our old friend Jack who drives *or* the accomplice who drives. The judge doesn't know and the prosecutor doesn't know. So when you use "nor" or "or," keep with two singular nouns and make the verb singular. The answer: A and D. By the way, if the subject is "neither" or "either," that verb still yearns to be singular. Look: "Neither of them has regrets." And not: "Neither of them have regrets."

7. The hang-up: I get it! So if I have two things in a list, like, let's say, a bicycle and a boat (both good for island travel, by the way), then the verb should be singular. What a relief, now I get it. (I think.)

Is this your hang-up? Take the test:

A. A bicycle and a boat are how he travels around the island.

B. A bicycle and a boat is how he travels around the island.

Here's the answer: Sorry, don't mean to confuse you. But remember, I didn't write the rules—just this book. The "and" in the sentence means you have two things, not just one, so the verb must be plural. "The bike and the boat are…" would be correct. Perhaps the answer would be more obvious if I wrote it this way: "A bicycle and a boat are excellent ways to travel around a small, luxurious island." But then, this wouldn't be much of a test, would it?

8. The hang-up: Okay, I get it now, really. So if I have two singular nouns joined by "and," I should use plural verbs because these two things are combined. That's easy. And if I have "neither" and "either," I should use a singular verb because they're separate. Let me focus on Derek for a minute. Say I'm writing about his bad habits (believe me, he has plenty). What happens if I have a singular noun like "gin" and a plural noun like "cigarettes," and connect them with "neither," "either," "nor," or "or"; what then?

Is this your hang-up? Take the test:

A. Either gin or cigarettes contributes to his steady decline.

B. Either gin or cigarettes contribute to his steady decline.

Here's the answer: Yes, I see the difficulty. In this kind of example, protocol counts. If you have a singular and plural, put the singular first in the sentence. Then, add the plural. The verb will conveniently take the plural form, and your answer will be B.

9. The hang-up: What if I interrupt the sentence with, say, "along with," "as well as," "besides," or "not," to add to the list of his vices?

Is this your hang-up? Take the test:

A. Gin, along with cigarettes and gambling, contributes to his steady decline.

B. Gin, along with cigarettes and gambling, contribute to his steady decline.

Here's the answer: Ignore anything that's parenthetical, in this case cigarettes and gambling. So you're really telling us that gin contributes to his decline, and A is correct.

10. The hang-up: Let's say I'm talking about Derek and me. Not that I would, you understand, but let's pretend. How would I word the sentence if I were to discuss a mutual interest of ours? Is this your hang-up? Take the test:

A. Neither the boys nor I am above a little financial creativity.
B. Neither the boys nor I are above a little financial creativity.

Here's the answer: Put the boys, creepy as they are, first, then add "I" and the verb that should flow naturally from it. So the correct answer: "Neither the boys nor I am above a little financial creativity."

A Brief Outburst Plus the Author's Response

The Outburst: Okay, look. You started this book off saying rules don't matter as much as those, what do you call 'em, Grammar Mavens, think. And now you're shoveling out all these rules. You know—who cares whether it's "are" or "is"—who knows the difference? Who the heck cares?

The Author's Response: Chill. I didn't say rules don't matter, I said they're changing. And yes, you can break rules, but only for two reasons: (1) The broken rules sound better than the alternatives. (2) People break the rule so often, the rule is becoming the exception in common usage.

Metaphor: The Powermonger

A Strategy Break

Metaphor is a really powerful tool for getting the right response from e-mails, ads, brochures, even your run-of-the-mill manuals. By the way, I don't mean metaphors such as "This manual is like a best friend guiding you through the darkness of uncertainty," but those built directly into your writing.

Let's start by breaking words into two groups: literal words and metaphors. Literal is exactly what it says:

Martha threw the pencil and it stuck in Gilbert's eye.

She really threw the pencil and really, it stuck in Gilbert's eye. But only for a moment. If you use "threw" as a metaphor, you might say:

Gilbert threw a temper tantrum, but later threw out the possibility of revenge since Martha didn't mean it.

In neither case did Gilbert actually throw anything. Here are a few more examples:

Quick Metaphor Cheat Sheet

Verb
1. follow
2. hurry
3. walk
4. hit

Literal
1. If you don't stop following me I'll call the police.
2. Tom hurried through the dumbbell exercises to be the first on the rowing machine.
3. Marsha, you look like a boy when you walk.
4. Tom, I feel like hitting you.

Metaphorical
1. I follow my desires wherever they lead me.
2. Oh, Tom, you're much too busy hurrying through life to enjoy it.
3. Let me walk you through the dumbbell safety tips.
4. That last comment really hit the point.

Business Writing: The Official Metaphor Application

So what does all this have to do with creating quick, painless and powerful business writing? Let's focus on verb metaphors, since we're in the verb section of this book and verbs, as I said, are the macho guys of the word-use kingdom: While tender at times, they love power, and your metaphors can give it to them.

Try this: Get a pencil. Oh, go ahead, it will only take a moment, and if you really want, don't bother with the paper. Just write on a napkin. Now, ready? Write everything you equate with the word "follow." My list would contain words like: "stay behind," "go after," "passive agreement." Not exactly power-inspiring.

So let's say you're e-mailing someone about a new technology system your company is implementing. If they don't use it correctly, then possibly the whole system will implode or hackers will steal their secrets. So naturally, you give a talk, send out e-mails, and insert warnings into your manual like: "You must follow these instructions."

To heat up the message, you might say: "IMPORTANT: You must follow these instructions." Still, the verb practically shrivels into oblivion. So what do you do instead? Good question. Lots of alternatives abound, including: "adhere to," "apply," "employ," "stick to", "abide by"...not the strongest, but better than "follow."

Another example is "give," as in: "Steve, will you give us your opinion?" That's okay; a little flat. Not exactly encouraging. So here are some others:

◆ "Steve, will you share your opinion?" Friendly, common to facilitators in heated circumstances such as management–union disputes, "share" stands among what I call the "Barney verbs": just hearing them makes you expect the purple dinosaur to walk in.

◆ "Steve, will you voice your opinion?" That's when Steve, a vocal union supporter, is quiet, in a passive-aggressive way. You know, twisting in his seat. Squirming. Sighing loudly. "Voice" empowers while commenting on his current behavior.

◆ "Steve, will you reveal your opinion?" Steve isn't saying a whole lot. No squirming, no body language. What *could* he be thinking?

◆ "Okay guys, why don't you start by throwing out some of your thoughts?" Actually, this option belongs at the beginning of the meeting. Unlike "throwing" a fit, "throwing out" your thoughts sounds ironic, almost fun, as in: "Okay, lets throw a ball around, enjoy ourselves, then get down to business."

Linking Verbs

Now, let's talk about linking verbs, aka the "to be" forms: "is," "are," "was," "were," "being," "been," "be," and the mother ship itself, "to be." They don't actually *do* anything, but they connect the noun to some feature:

◆ *Miss Ferguson* is *probably* old *by now.*

◆ *The cafeteria food* was dreadful.

◆ *What* is *the* cost *of cafeteria food today?*

You can't "is." You can't "was." No—in the color scheme of word use, action verbs glow with flashing neon lights while dreary little verb bits have the vibrancy of cement gray. They serve one function alone: They link. Look at these other examples of linking verbs:

◆ *Arthur* is *one of those guys who likes to jump off high places.*

◆ *Arthur* was *rather peculiar as a kid.*

◆ *Arthur's mother, Sal,* is *the owner of Betty's Grille 'n' Grease.*

So What About Them?

Everyone loves high-energy action verbs. Yet those linking verbs creep in, dulling the sentence anyway. So what's a busy business-person to do? Look at these alternatives—consider them literary Viagra. Don't stress, but apply them when you can:

Use adjectives before the noun—not after. Let's take the example: "Arthur is our neighbor." Now suppose the next sentence was: "He once jumped off the shopping mall roof." You could say "Our neighbor Arthur jumped off the shopping mall roof" instead.

Here are a few more:

Linking: "The mall director is Rupert Shoeman. He said Arthur landed on a box of ornamental wreaths."

Not linking: "Mall director Rupert Shoeman said Arthur landed on a box of ornamental wreaths."

Linking: "The shoppers were surprised. They grabbed the kids and headed for their cars."

Not linking: "The surprised shoppers grabbed their kids and headed for their cars."

Use qualifiers between commas. Similar idea as the last. So instead of saying: "Rupert Shoeman was once a doctor. He lived in New York." Try: "Rupert Shoeman, a former doctor, lived in New York."

Linking: "The children were in the Christmas spirit. They thought Arthur was Santa Claus."

Not linking: "The children, in the Christmas spirit, thought Arthur was Santa Claus."

Linking: "The kids were little, probably three or four years old. They looked like elves."

Not linking: "The kids, probably three or four years old, looked like elves."

Find an action verb to replace the linking verb. Action verbs work well as linking verb replacements. So instead of saying: "Laurie, the shoe saleswoman, *was* bored by the whole event." You could say: "Laurie, the shoe saleswoman, *felt* bored by the whole event."

Linking: "Laurie *is* a shopping queen."

Not linking: "Laurie *reigns* as a shopping queen."

Linking: "The shoes *are* unusual."

Not linking: "The shoes *stand out.*"

To Be—But for How Long?

There's much debate in the language kingdom about the linking verb. Some advocate that stylebooks limit it to a certain percentage—the way they limit the acceptable quantity of the passive voice. Others cry that the English language no longer needs it, while others ignore the discussion altogether. Stay tuned as the teeth gnashing continues...

Q&P Break: The Dare

Take a look at something you've recently written. If you've used "to be" more than two times in every paragraph, go through and start adjusting. Do this for practice, and if you have time, do it for real. Eventually, you'll break the linking verb habit.

Helping Verbs

Beware of the helping verb/linking verb confusion. Sure the words look the same, but they have distinctly different functions. The linking verbs, as we said, link. The helping verbs help. Let's look at the linking verb "is." As in: "Rupert *is* the Salvation Army Santa." The word transforms into a helping verb in a sentence like this one: "Rupert *is working* long hours this holiday season." Now, the "is" helps the word "working," so it means Rupert *is working* over a long period of time.

Other helping verbs include:

◆ **will:** "Rupert *will be working* long hours over Valentine's Day weekend when he dresses up as Cupid."

◆ **has:** "Rupert *has dressed* up as the Thanksgiving Turkey, and on July 4th, Uncle Sam."

◆ **were:** "We *were impressed* by how much Cupid looked like Santa."

Helping Verb–Linking Verb Cheat Sheet

Helping Verb
We are dying to eat pizza.
Mr. Stoller is working hard tonight.
Mr. Sroller is eating pizza at his desk.
The Stollers are rushing around today.

Linking Verb
We are pizza lovers.
Mr. Stoller is a hard worker.
Mr. Stoller is messy.
The Stollers are a busy family.

Adverbs: Too Much, Too Often

Adverbs are touchy words. Yes, you need them, but in moderation only. They're rather like cologne—a dab is great, but a splash overwhelms. In case you've forgotten, adverbs describe verbs and are most famous for their "-ly" endings. So you might say:

She typed quickly, although the phone was busily ringing and her cell phone was vibrating mercilessly, all frantically trying desperately to get her attention.

Adverbs also describe adjectives and other adverbs. Let's look at two of the least savory ones:

◆ **Very.** Someone should nominate "very" for the most useless word of the millennium. It sounds boring and provides absolutely *no* meaning at all. If you learn that Billy Rider, an employee, is "very difficult," would you omit him from your team, but let him join if he were just "difficult"? I find the double verys especially annoying, like when people say: "We're having a very, VERY big problem, so stay away!" As

Mark Twain once advised: "Substitute 'damn' every time you're inclined to write 'very'; your editor will delete it and the writing will be just as it should be."

◆ **Really.** By "really," I mean to imply a degree. As in "a really hot item." Or "I really want you to come." And why is "really" unsavory? Everything I said about "very." Only one exception: when you mean "really" to mean honestly, or actually, as in: "He really is coming this time."

The real problem with "very" and "really": they're the dumb blondes of writing: quick, easy, but not a whole lot of substance. So what do you do? 'Fess up. Tell all by using specifics such as: "We're having a 50–75 percent OFF sale" or "Billy Rider has a habit of punching people in the face when they don't agree with him." Then they'll catch your meaning—he's more than difficult.

As for those other adverbs—moderation is *key*. And beware:

Steer clear of obvious adverbs. One example: "Stanley ran through the assignments quickly." How can someone run *slowly*? What choice did Stanley have? Or how about: "Stanley worked steadily from 8:00 to 8:00." If he worked from 8:00 to 8:00 then yes, he worked steadily. Or this all-time favorite: "Stanley works hard to bring excellent customer service." Well, okay, but would we say: "Stanley only works a wee bit" to give excellent customer service? Hardly.

Never use an adverb where a verb will do. Let's go back to Stanley running quickly. Maybe you *do* want to show that he ran faster than your normal trot. Avoid the adverb and try: "Stanley raced," or "Stanley zoomed," or "Stanley rushed."

Adverb Cheat Sheet

Plus a Verb Replacement List

Adverb/Verb	Verb replacements
moved quickly	hurried, rushed, hustled
laughed hard	guffawed, roared, hooted
worked steadily	labored, struggled, plowed ahead
reviewed carefully	examined, analyzed, zoned in
accurately changed	adjusted, adapted, corrected, fine-tuned
stepped softly	tiptoed, breezed, skulked, snuck

Chapter 5
Glue Words

We call prepositions and conjunctions "glue words" because they stick bits and pieces of your sentence together so they make sense. They're easy to use—no messy tense to worry about, no person agreements to negotiate, no pressing parallelism to consider...well, maybe some, but nothing major. By now you must know, as the comedienne Gilda Radner once said: "It's always something." First, though, The Review.

The Review

Conjunction Functions

Most people remember conjunctions from grammar school—how can you forget? They were everywhere. They were friendly.

Look, who struggles to learn the meaning of the word "and"? And "but" is a real snap. Besides, "conjunction" rhymes so well, it's become the poster child for good grammar everywhere, like the "Conjunction Junction" episode of *Schoolhouse Rock*. Here's a list of some conjunctions to jog your memory:

Conjunction Cheat Sheet

accordingly	after	also
although	as	as if
as though	assuming that	because
before	consequently	even if
even though	furthermore	hence
how	however	if
in case	in order that	instead
likewise	meanwhile	moreover
nevertheless	otherwise	once
provided that	rather	since that
still	then	therefore
though	unless	until
whenever	where	wherever

Conjunctions: The Review

Let's review: for, and, nor, but, or, yet, so

Remember the name for these? Does "coordinating conjunction" ring a bell? Or maybe you remember them by the acronym English lovers everywhere love using: "FANBOYS"—as in For, And, Nor, But, Or, Yet, So. Sounds almost threatening, doesn't it—like a street gang? These little guys join two sentences, words, thoughts, or ideas. You might say:

We heard the FANBOYS were coming to town, so we decided to lie low for a while.

Margaret stayed indoors the whole time, but Ray and Phil headed out for supplies.

Even the local Grammar Mavens regarded their arrival with fear and dread.

The 'ands' are okay, but never trust a 'yet'.

Let's review: After, although, as, as if, as long as, as though, because, before, even if, even though, if, if only, in order that, now that, once, rather than, since, so that, than, that

"Subordinating conjunctions"; these words make one part of the sentence that depends on the rest to have meaning. Notice some of the prepositions make an appearance as conjunctions as well:

Even though I travel constantly, I'm terrified of planes.

Once, during turbulence, I grabbed the guy next to me.

Although stunned, he was polite.

The Case of Then and Than

Let's end the confusion right now between "than" and "then."

Than: when you compare two people or things: "I'd rather hitchhike *than* fly."

Then: when one event follows from another: "I grabbed the guy next to me, *then* held on tight."

Let's review: Either...or; neither...nor; not only...but also; whether...or; both...and

These guys—called "correlative conjunctions"—usually travel in pairs. They're monogamous so don't try matching them with anything else. Here are some examples:

Not only did he blush, but he also giggled.

Both the flight attendants and the other passengers suspected the worst.

Never Use Three Where One Will Do

Sure, conjunctions are easy to remember, but they're pretty milquetoast. How exciting can "and," "but," and "neither–nor" get? So rather than say:

His office was cluttered with magazines and videos and books for the Golden-Age set.

try:

His office was cluttered with magazines, videos, and books for the Golden Age set.

Unless of course, your message looks like this:

Just by joining our Golden Age Club you'll get free magazines and videos and books.

Prepositions: The Review Two

Prepositions indicate a direction: **on, over, above, under, before, after.** If it takes you there, it's a preposition. Let's take the verb "crush," in a sentence such as this:

Martin crushed the walnut.

Where did he crush it? What happened? That's where the preposition comes in:

Martin crushed the walnut in his fist.

Martin crushed the walnut on the keyboard.

Martin crushed the walnut under his car.

Forget your prepositions? No problem, just consult this handy cheat sheet:

Preposition Cheat Sheet

about	above	according to
across	after	against
around	at	because of
before	behind	below
beneath	beside	besides
between	beyond	by
by way of	down	during
except	for	from
in	in addition to	in front of
in place of	in regard to	in spite of
inside	instead of	into
like	near	of
off	on	on account of
out	out of	outside
over	since	through
throughout	to	toward
under	until	up
upon	with	without

So why are prepositions so easy to use? Exposure. Hardly an utterance goes by that doesn't contain a preposition. You just use them naturally. But do you *exploit* them to your absolute advantage in business documents? That is the question. Here's what to do:

◆ Hide them, mostly. As with conjunctions, the less the reader notices them, the better. You probably do this instinctively anyway, so rather than say:

The FANBOYS infiltrated everything: They appeared on our cereal boxes, on the radio, and on the bulletin board at work.

try:

The FANBOYS infiltrated everything: They appeared on our cereal boxes, radio, and bulletin board at work.

But if you need different prepositions for your list, include them all:

Hide if you want to—at your desk, in your car, within the bowels of your bedroom—nowhere is safe.

◆ Set a rhythm. At times, you *do* want to overuse prepositions—especially to establish a rhythm within the sentence:

The FANBOYS—sure, you fear and loath them, but sometimes you need them: In those show tunes you play in the car, in that e-mail you send to your boss, even in the words that whisper in your head.

◆ Opt for "up," "over," and "out" prepositions, and when you have a choice; steer clear of "down" ones. In our society "up" words have good connotations and "down" words have bad. Think about your job. Do you want to move up or down? Same thing with forwards and backwards. Do you want to move ahead or fall behind?

Granted, we're talking detail here, and the difference may be minute. But in the business world, if the advantage is yours, grab it. So when writing a proposal:

◆ **Don't do:** "Let's get down to basics…"
And why: Unless you're dancing, who wants to get down to anything? Down is low, un-important. We're professionals—we're above all that.
How about: "Let's focus on core issues…" Or how about: "Let's start with…"

◆ **Don't do:** "Everyone contributes to our customer service, from the highest ranking VP down to the lowest level employees."
And why: Oh great. I'm sure the "lowest level employees" really appreciate that.

How about: "Everyone contributes to our customer service, from leading VPs to front line employees."

◆ **Don't do:** "You have to dumb down your language so everyone can understand it."
And why: This is a personal favorite—we'll explore more when we get to the section on plain language. For now, suffice it to say, this little line stokes up images of the groveling worker, face covered with the dirt of low-level toil, too dumb to grasp even the most rudimentary point. So scratch "down," and then scratch "dumb."
How about: "You have to open up your language so it's accessible to everyone."

Preposition Problems?

Have preposition problems? Could be you suffer from under-exposure, as if you communicate primarily through American Sign Language (ASL) or if English is your second language. So remember the magic formula: read, read, read. And write, write, write, and get a preposition check every day. Eventually they'll start slipping into place. Conjunctions and Prepositions: The Controversy Begins!

Glue Words Controversy #1: Conjunction Consumption

The controversy: whether or not to start a sentence with a conjunction. Grammar Mavens vote no. Common sense votes yes.

It could be that your conjunctions are suffering from consumption—not only because the combination "conjunction" and "consumption" rhymes so nicely, but also because your conjunctions may be sick. And why? Because you're wedging them into the darkness of the paragraph, insisting they simply join words, phrases, and sentences and never see the bright and nourishing light that you can only find in the beginning of a sentence.

But forget the conjunction for a minute. What about you? Are you getting the full value of your conjunctions? Or are you squeamish about breaking the "never start a sentence with a conjunction" rule? Or perhaps you think the sentences just sound wrong with that conjunction shamelessly exposed up front. If so, reread this paragraph—I started three of the sentences with a conjunction, and you probably didn't notice.

Here's another example, just to press the point:

The Buried Conjunction

You're moving along in the paragraph and the sentences flow nice and smooth. The reader starts getting drowsy because everything is a little *too* nice and smooth. You could add exciting verbs or interesting sentences or even break that rhythm a little by starting with conjunctions. Unfortunately you can't, because the "rules" won't allow it. No problem; your reader is asleep.

Think you should start sentences with conjunctions only followed by perky messages? Don't worry. They work for messages of fear, distress, and everyday concern too. See what I mean:

You have several problems these days when trying to please your reader. This generic person doesn't like to read. They're overwhelmed with messages. And they have a 10-second attention span. So what can you do?

Glue Words Controversy #2

The controversy: whether to end a sentence with a preposition. You know what the Grammar Mavens think, don't you?

We already touched on the question of whether you can put the preposition at the end of a sentence, so let's clear this up once and for all, and move on. *Yes*, you *can* put a preposition at the end of a sentence. It's okay. *Unless* you are writing a highly formal document or your reader will take notice—keep in mind that while most people are okay with this construction, some people in the business world are as bad as the Grammar Mavens, so know who you're talking to. But for the most part, why *not* put the preposition at the end of the sentence? It sounds more natural than many of the alternatives, anyway.

◆ No preposition: "To whom does this Sondheim sound book belong?

- Yes preposition: "Who does this Sondheim sound book belong to?"

- No preposition: "It was a gift—you'll never believe from whom I got it."

- Yes preposition: "It was a gift—you'll never believe who I got it from."

- No preposition: "Did Jack send it from the secret island on which he is living?"

- Yes preposition: "Did Jack send it from the secret island he is living on?"

- No preposition: "Actually the FANBOYS sent it—inside they even put a nice note."

- Yes preposition: "Actually the FANBOYS sent it—they even put a nice note inside."

Last Word: Preposition Past

Here's what *The American Heritage Book of English Usage, A Practical and Authoritative Guide to Contemporary English* (1996) tells us about the history of this controversy:

> It was John Dryden, the 17th-century poet and dramatist, who first promulgated the doctrine that a preposition may not be used at the end of a sentence. Grammarians in the 18th century refined the doctrine, and the rule has since become one of the most venerated maxims of schoolroom grammar. But sentences ending with prepositions can be found in the works of most of the great writers since the Renaissance. In fact, English syntax not only allows, but sometimes even requires, final placement of the preposition, as in, "We have much to be thankful for," or "That depends on what you believe in." Efforts to rewrite such sentences to place the preposition elsewhere can have comical results, as Winston Churchill demonstrated when he objected to the doctrine by saying "This is the sort of English up with which I cannot put."

Chapter 6
Sentence Savvy

Now for sentences. No mere assemblies of words, sentences are a font of power. Think I'm being dramatic? I'm not. Sentences can induce moods faster than a Xanax and engender responses so subtle and real that, if you got really good at this, you'd be dangerous...and probably in advertising. Anyway, we'll start with simple sentences, the snub-nosed pistol in your arsenal of powerful sentences.

But First! An Answer to the Eternal Sentence Question

Here's the question: How long should the average sentence be? I'm sure you've asked it. Maybe you've answered it. Over the years, I've heard *lots* of responses. Among the many:

♦ **No longer than you can say in one breath.** I heard this one in college. It makes sense, I suppose...I mean, anything longer would be marathon length. Still, not all breathers are the same. So by this reasoning, asthmatic people should have sentences of, say, five or 10 words, maximum, since they take shallow breaths but more of them; and athletes, with impressive lung capacity, can have sentences of say, 50-plus words per sentence. As for the stressed-out people, the ones who *forget* to breathe, sentences could potentially go on for paragraphs, or until they pass out.

♦ **Keep them short.** Great idea, given your reader's short attention span. Really, who has the wherewithal to endure for more than a one-line sentence anyway? Only problem: short sentences sound choppy. They can be irritating. They have the potential to bore the reader. So short is out. Definitely out.

♦ **Stick to about a line and a half.** You have the same problem that you had with choppy sentences, in which you have similar length over and over. The reader does not want sameness, because sameness is boring and distracting. People take vacations and watch a variety of movies to *break* the sameness. I am using the line-and-a-half strategy now, so this paragraph probably sounds less effective than the rest.

So what is the *real* answer? Think rhythm. Think variety. Think sound. Listen to a Beethoven symphony. It's not just the notes, but the rhythm that slows you down, hurriesyouup, stops...then starts again. Beethoven, Green Day, Sondheim, or Britney Spears: it's all about the rhythm, man.

Make no mistake; writing has a rhythm too. When you use one sentence length, you create a monotonous sound. Granted, in music, monotony *can* pay off—like Gregorian chants or Philip Glass. Their music has a mesmerizing effect. But who wants to be mesmerized by writing? Intrigued? Excited? Involved? Interested? Sure. But not mesmerized. So think long, short-short, long, long, short, long, stop.

The Assembly: Sentence Types

Simple Sentences

Let's start with the anatomy of a simple sentence. You have one actor—be it a person, a group of people, a thing, or lots of things—doing one action or one set of actions. So your sentence looks like this:

Noun–Verb

Janette wore bright red hiking boots.

Your simple sentences can contain more information. Like this:

Janette wore bright red hiking boots on the nude beach.

You have the person doing the action, "Janette," and the action, "wore." Here are some other simple sentences:

Arnold watched Janette.

He wanted a peek at Janette's toes.

Janette's boots looked like overgrown tomatoes in the scorching sun.

The Actor-less Simple Sentence: aka The Imperative

Some sentences don't require the noun–verb structure we mentioned earlier. If you have kids, you know them well—they're commands. As in "Clean your room this instant!" You don't have to say: "Mike, clean your room," because little Mike knows you're talking to him. Here are some other examples:

Help please!

Look out!

Danger ahead!

Or more typical of the business world:

Payment due.

Quick, a customer!

These little guys are great for instructions too. People want to work on the actual project—whether setting up a new security system or heating a can of soup—and not the instructions on how to do it. So keep it quick; keep it clean.

Simple Sentence Strategies Revisited

The concept of "keep it simple, keep it simple" is great—it does the heart good and I'm in favor of it. But remember: too many simple sentences sound choppy. They sound monotonous. They tend to have lots of repetition. They can drive you crazy. Get the idea?

So think Chinese water torture: drip-drip-drip. Then mix and match the simple sentence with longer ones, depending on the meaning you want to project.

And Now...The Exceptions

As for the exceptions—they're those snub-nosed pistols I mentioned earlier. Firearms, nudity, and Chinese torture...who ever said business writing was dull? Anyway, when you do it right, short sentences also infuse your message with urgency, excitement, and energy. Compare, if you will:

Short and urgent:

Ned and I need the survival kit! Please—send it immediately. Poisonous snakes lurk everywhere. If you do not treat a bite immediately, paralysis will set in. The natives use berry juice and spit. We want something stronger!

Longish sentences:

Ned and I need the survival kit and would appreciate your sending it to us immediately. Poisonous snakes lurk everywhere and if you don't treat a bite immediately, paralysis will set in. The natives use berry juice and spit, but we want something stronger.

Simple sentences also propel electronic messages—from e-mails to Websites—in which people naturally expect speed and power.

Let's look at e-mails for a minute. Think of them as a cross between a Blackberry message and a voice mail. You have to add more than a few words, but don't want to ramble. Compare these examples—one long, and one short with a little nip and tuck on the word use:

Longish:

> *Deb Ryan contacted me about the plans for the demolition of the old farmhouse for the new Esquire Property. Protesters from the Preservation Society are picketing and someone from the Farmers Association has strapped himself to the silo, so we're not sure what to do. Calling the police will just bring in bad press, reinforce some of the negative publicity we've had in the past, and lower the value of the properties. So we want to know what you think we should do.*

Shortish:

> *Help! Deb Ryan just called about demolishing the old farmhouse for the new Esquire Property. Protesters from the Preservation Society are picketing! Someone from the Farmers Association has strapped himself to the silo! Can't call the police—they'll just bring in bad press and reinforce past negative publicity. It will lower the property value. What should we do?*

Even your ordinary e-mail has more pizzazz when short sentences kick in:

Longish:

> *I need the materials for the Colbert proposal by noon today and would appreciate it if you sent them to me. It's also important that you know this matter is urgent.*

Shortish:

> *Urgent: send the materials for the Colbert proposal by noon today, please.*

Also kick in those simple sentences when writing other speed-addicted documents including ads, job postings, announcements, posters, how-tos, and blogs.

The Compound Sentence: Siamese Twins

You can compare compound sentences to Siamese twins: They're two (or more) simple sentences joined at the conjunction. Here's how they look:

Sentence 1 *Bob is fond of making controversial statements*
Sentence 2 *...although he chronically gets in trouble.*

Sentence 1 *We suspect Bob wrote on the bathroom wall*
Sentence 2 *...but Bob denies this fiercely.*

Sentence 1 *Fran said the comments were interesting*
Sentence 2 *...because they contained stock tips.*

Q&P Break

Compound Addiction: Take out a document you wrote recently. Look at the sentences. Probably you use compound sentences more than any others. That's because you know that simple sentences annoy the reader and long sentences bore them, so you probably go for compound sentences. They're sort of similar to a middle child—correct and eager to please. If this is true, concentrate on sentence variety—throw in some of those simple sentences, blend in some of the complex and compound–complex we'll talk about in a minute.

The Complex Sentence

Complex sentences are similar to some marriages I know. One partner mercilessly depends on the other for his or her identity and very meaning in the world. In complex sentence terms, we call this person the "dependent clause," which looks something like this:

After he read the stock tips on the wall...

Doesn't make sense, right? Round it off with a simple sentence, aka "independent clause":

Arnold changed his investment strategies.

Together, they make a charming set:

Dependent clause   *After he read the stock tips on the wall,*
Independent clause   *...Arnold changed his investment strategies.*

Of course, you can always start with the independent clause. Look:

Whenever I read his messages, I practically get goose bumps.

I practically get goose bumps whenever I read his messages.

These guys are great for variety, breaking the monotony of your average simple or compound sentence. Even better, they help you position a riveting but indirectly related matter up front where it belongs:

After he lost a cool $1 million in Enron stocks, Arnold was glad for the tips.

Compound–Complex Sentences

What can you say about compound–complex sentences? They're simple sentences dressed to the max thanks to compound and complex adornments. Very chic. Very professional. But not for just any occasion—and most definitely *not* more than once per paragraph.

Compound:

He watched Janette in her red boots and he longingly considered her feet.

Complex:

As Arnold relaxed on the beach,...

Compound–Complex:

As Arnold relaxed on the beach, he watched Janette in her red boots and he longingly considered her feet.

Compound:

Janette made a killing on the market because she followed sound advice.

Complex:

Although she was fiercely independent,...

Compound–Complex:

Although she was fiercely independent, Janette made a killing on the market because she followed sound advice.

Sentence Bits and Pieces for the Maximum Effect

We've covered the big sentence structure items; now for sentence structure bits and pieces with plenty of "do's and don'ts" tips—a must in business-writing books.

Phrases

As with a dependent clause, a phrase can not stand alone. Here's an example:

At the Anti-Graffiti Society meeting...

What about the Anti-Graffiti Society meeting? What happened? Who was involved? This pseudo-sentence begs for meaning and you'll find it in none other than our friendly independent clause:

At the Anti-Graffiti Society meeting, Hazel Hawksworth read her letter to Representative Hollington.

What is the difference between a dependent clause and a phrase? The dependent clause contains a noun and a verb; the phrase contains one *or* the other. That's all.

Do: Use phrases to start a sentence. They add the variety your reader loves and give you a chance to play around with structure. **Do:** Use unattached phrases when appropriate. These daring alternatives work well in ads, e-mails, and marketing materials of all sizes and stripes. Just be sure you do it right so that the phrase intrigues the reader, not distracts them. Here's an example:

Ms. Hawksworth claimed graffiti is the new national epidemic. It's on public buildings. On street signs. Inside and outside the subway.

Don't: Distract the reader with phrases that stand out like red boots on a nude beach—or worse, appear to be a mistake.

Fragments: These sentence structure bits hang around the paragraph. Maybe they're phrases. Maybe they're clauses. Maybe you intended them to be there. Maybe not. Here's an example:

Because she's devoted to the cause.

So here's the approach:

Do: "Hazel campaigns tirelessly. Why? Because she's devoted to the cause."

Don't: Same as with phrases.

Appositives. Save your most important point for last, so the reader races through the sentence, stops at the colon, then BAM: reads the key words. Here are two examples:

Do:

During the meeting, she had one thing in her mind: spray paint.

Our Ever-Clean Cleanser takes away the toughest stain of all: graffiti.

One person matters most to the team at Ever-Clean: Hazel.

Misplaced Modifiers

These troublesome sentence faux pas are easy to overlook. Here's an example:

Although happy to spend the day relaxing, the graffiti in the city beckoned and Hazel got to work.

Notice how the first part of the sentence doesn't say *who* is happy to relax. The first word of the independent clause should divulge. But what's this? Graffiti? The *graffiti* is happy to relax? Don't think so. This is the rewrite:

> *Although happy to spend the day relaxing, Hazel grabbed her Ever-Clean cleanser and got to work on the graffiti in the city.*

The do's: No do's. Just don't.

The don'ts: The reasoning behind this rule goes as follows: The misplaced modifier can confuse readers, especially in more complicated sentences. Besides, most people recognize that you made a mistake, and pay attention to the mistake—not what you're saying.

Run-on sentences: That's when you have a sentence that goes on and on and on and you can tell if you have a run-on because the thoughts go on for longer than a sane person would permit and tires you just to think about so don't do it.

The do's: Run-on sentences will knock your opponent into submission.

The don'ts: Don't. Really. Just don't.

Don't Forget These Strategies:

Short sentences in a row. You use short, simple sentences to create the jarring feel we discussed about the urgent message. Here's how it looks:

> *Send the Ever-Clean! I need it by 5:00. Any later, and it will be too late! The ink will set!*

Short words in a row. Use this device on *rare* occasions only, and remember they'll give your average Grammar Maven a seizure. They can be helpful, though, in certain situations such as this:

> *Dry marker. Paint. Coal. The graffiti artists use so much, but say so little.*

Bullets. Have three or more important points? Use bullets so the reader can see them.

Rumor Has It...Could This Be You?

Rumor has it that comma splices are the most common sentence structure mistake around. Sadly, comma splices are like bad breath. They're obvious and unpleasant, although no fault of the inflicted person. So check and see if the problem is yours.

Here's what you look for: Two sentences joined with a comma. The comma simply is not strong enough to hold them together and the structure sags, as you can see here:

Hazel received a grant from the Ever-Clean Foundation, she received a matching gift from the National Society of Grammar Mavens who were outraged at the prevalence of foul word use.

Here's what you do about it: Lots of choices here.

Choice 1: Join them with a conjunction (and cut a bit, if you're so inclined):

Hazel received a grant from the Ever-Clean Foundation and a matching gift from the National Society of Grammar Mavens, who were outraged at the prevalence of foul word use.

Choice 2: Join them with a colon or semi-colon (a unique way of joining sentences your reader can't help but appreciate):

Hazel received a grant from the Ever-Clean Foundation; she received a matching gift from the National Society of Grammar Mavens. They were outraged at the prevalence of foul word use.

Choice 3: Separate them with a period (a common but useful option depending on what you want for rhythm):

Hazel received a grant from the Ever-Clean Foundation. She also received a matching gift from the National Society of Grammar Mavens, who were outraged at the prevalence of foul word use.

Q&P Break

Now, while this chapter is fresh in your mind, take out a document you just wrote or write a new one. If possible, use a real-life document for work. E-mails are great. Website pieces—also great. If you happen to be in public relations, go ahead and grab that news release.

Then write the piece for content. Don't worry about the sentences just yet.

Go back and use at least two of the sentence possibilities we discussed here—appositives, short sentences in a row, whatever you choose, in each paragraph.

Rewrite. Remember: Take risks. Experiment. Play around. You're not building a nuclear bomb; you're writing a business document, so have some fun with it.

Q&P Break

What is your sentence structure problem? The comma splices we discussed moments ago? Misplaced modifiers? Whatever it is, you probably can't see it. I mean, no one *deliberately* makes mistakes when they write, correct? So get your writing coach to check for sentence structure mistakes. Then check-and-correct and watch the mistakes melt away.

Quick, Painless, and Plain:
Almost All You Need to Know About Style

Chapter 7
Plain Language Primer:
So What Are the Big Guys Afraid Of?

Writing business documents? Think plain language. It's *the* only way to get the right response from the reader, no matter who that person might be: a guy on the street, a close friend, or a senior vice president with four Ph.D.s.

Naturally, plain language is steeped in controversy, mindless and ludicrous as that controversy might be. I discovered this firsthand as part of the White House initiative on plain language under the Clinton-Gore administration. Among other tasks, I trained thousands and thousands and *thousands* of employees on plain language, and heard innumerable opinions in the process. The experience was similar to jumping through a minefield—plenty of safe, friendly spots, but you never knew when you might get your foot blown off.

Before we get into the details—sordid and otherwise—let's look at the anatomy of plain language. In essence, you do five things—all so practical and wholesome, even Miss Ferguson would embrace them:

1. **Use the active voice.** That means a clear relationship between who did what in the sentence. A no-brainer, right? The arch-nemesis of the active voice is the passive voice; sinister, but easy to control.

2. **Keep word use concise.** I know this sounds so obvious it's almost boring, but it's true. Most business writing is so weighed down in extra words, you'd think the computer where it's housed would die of obesity.

3. **Reader-focus.** The brainchild of advertisers every-where, reader-focus gives the reader information that's important to them in a style they can handle. That includes visuals too, such as charts, graphs, and white space so clear and bright, you almost forget you're reading.

4. **Accessible tone.** This is where the "dumbing down" thing comes in. People confuse a tangled, arrogant, or otherwise unlikable tone with a professional one. Not so. A clear and readable tone suits all knowl-edge sizes—from professionals to novices, without sacrificing your professional flair.

5. **Cohesive structure.** All this means is that one piece flows to the next. It's your basic Miss Ferguson lesson, minus the frosted pink lipstick and the five-paragraph essay.

All this is very nice indeed, only why bother? I don't just mean the federal government, I mean anyone. Private sector. Small businesses. You. The answer is the benefits, baby, the benefits. So many that the question really becomes "Why *not* bother?" Here are just a few:

Top Reasons You, Your Boss, Your Employees, Your Friends, and Yes, Even Your Attorneys, Should Use Plain Language at Work

◆ **The response you get from the reader.** As you know, you write to get the reader to do, think, feel, or otherwise respond to what you've written. No question, plain language will help you get that response in record time—assuming it's a response worth getting.

◆ **Your writing time.** Plain language is your natural voice, so once you give yourself an okay to use it, you'll speed up your writing time. Trust me—I've seen it with clients countless times.

◆ **Efficiency for your organization.** Plain language can speed up cycle time and decrease associated costs enormously. One Navy study, conducted in the late 1990s as part of the government's ongoing efforts to create readable text available to all citizens, shows that plain language significantly reduces reading and comprehension time, and so could save them between $250 and $350 million a year—for internal documents alone!

◆ **Better customer service for the customer—less time, expense, and heartbreak for you.** Other studies show plain language can cut questions from confused readers radically—in one private sector office, calls with questions about a computer manual dropped from around 50 a week to only three or four calls a month.

◆ **Better relations with your manager, reviewer, and Grammar Mavens everywhere.** With plain language, you standardize your approach, adding whatever quirky exceptions or words as necessary. With everyone in agreement, the review cycle floats by.

◆ **More reliable content.** Take out that jargon, those archaic legal terms, and countless other confusions, and guess what? You unearth the real meaning or content, which may not be content at all. So what is it? Let's say non-content. The writing just doesn't say anything. My employees and I discovered this firsthand: Roughly 75 percent of the thousands of pages of regulatory and policy documents we examined over 10 or so years made no sense at all.

◆ **Train without the trainer...**or training rooms, software, and that guy in the cubicle around the corner. The scenario goes like this: You have a question. The answer in the company manual is too garbled to understand, but no problem—the manual is so hard to navigate you never get there anyway. You want to ask your manager, but she's on an all-day conference call with the people at the home office. Besides, your manager is going to write your performance evaluation *and* recommend you for a promotion (or not), so do you really want to divulge what you *don't* know? So instead, you ask Hal in the corner cubicle. He's a bright guy and has been with the company forever.

Now let's step back a bit and look at a particular and peculiar aspect of human behavior. Say I ask you a question such as: "What's the weather going to be like tomorrow?" You don't know—you're not a meteorologist—hey, even the meteorologists don't know. But do you say, "I have no idea"? No. You look at the sky and say: "It probably will rain." Or: "The clouds will probably pass. I wouldn't worry about rain," or whatever.

Amazingly, people dispense wisdom far removed from their experience simply because someone asked. I have received countless tips on relieving sore muscles from my housekeeper and advice on child-rearing from everyone else—except my son's pediatrician, who avoids the subject. Ask Hal in the corner cubicle a question, and he'll answer it, whether he knows what he's talking about or not. And you'd be amazed at how often the answer is "not." Then you, grateful and relieved, follow his advice.

This scenario plays out endlessly in the workplace. But don't blame the employees—or the helpful Hals answering their questions. They can't help it. If only...if only they had a reliable manual to give them advice. To show them direction. To answer their questions with information that was correct and made sense. If only...they had plain language...

So Do You Use Plain Language?

Yes, you do. Not all the time, but when you think no one's looking. Take e-mails. Those very people whose proposals read similar to this:

Further, utilization of our full resources and development of solutions on a customer-needs basis assures that central issues are being addressed and modifications to old systems occur so benchmarks are reached...

write e-mails such as this:

Hey Ted, we're saved. We got the funding! No one has to go job hunting or go on unemployment.

Plain Language: The Sordid Details

The Q&P Tell-All Section

So why all the controversy? The reality reeks of, shall we say, unwholesome practices. Between you and me, I'm tempted to use words such as "unethical" and "unscrupulous," but I don't want to sound overly dramatic. Besides, this is a book on business writing, not consumer rights.

The most common reason people dislike plain language comes down to basic fallacies—not really immoral but definitely annoying. The argument goes two ways.

Argument #1: The most common—also the most ludicrous. It goes like this: "We have to write it this way..." And: "We've always written it this way..." And: "This is just how we do it." Yes, they desperately cling to the old way, which is about as practical as using a horse and buggy.

Argument #2: Plain language means "dumbing down" the message so everyone can understand it. This dumbing-down idea is nonsense. Does *The Wall Street Journal* or *The New York Times* dumb down its messages? Those publications use plain language. What the people who call plain language "dumbing down" are really saying: "If they don't know our language, they're not part of our club and can't have our information." The irony, as I've discovered over the years, is much of the time they don't understand their own language, either.

As for the unethical reasons? I'm thinking now of a series of meetings I conducted with representatives from numerous health plans about rewriting their brochures so the consumer can understand what they're getting. Sadly, the representatives couldn't make the content clear because they weren't sure what it meant. So they returned to home base, where their bosses and attorneys didn't know either, or welcomed the ambiguity—that way, if you asked for something they promised, they could say they didn't actually promise it.

Or how about those times during the plain language initiative, when administrative law judges insisted that plain language would undermine their authority because, as one judge put it: "We want loopholes with the law." Loopholes. In regulations. Or how about this marketing campaign in which a senior vice president informed me that: "If people knew what we were really selling, they wouldn't buy it." If I were senior VP and knew what they were really selling, I'd probably quit.

So why am I telling you all this? Because, my friends, plain language will help your business writing and your business life. And no matter what they say, there's no good reason *not* to use it.

Your Tax Dollars and Plain Language: The Mix

Bill Clinton loved plain language—Al Gore embraced it. And why? According to Gore, our democracy depends on it. Here's the reasoning: How can citizens know what to vote for unless they understand the laws they create? Not that citizens actually read the stuff. They simply wouldn't understand it. Which is his point, I guess.

Let's move on to how you can achieve plain language—starting with the two hottest items on the list: the active voice and concise word use.

Chapter 8
Why the Active Voice Isn't,
and a Few Words About Being Concise

As I wrote earlier, most people know they should use the active voice, and they know the passive voice is bad, bad, bad. Yet they have no idea about the difference between the passive and active voice—and have trouble figuring it out when active-inclined people try to explain it to them.

One problem rests in the name. With "passive," you probably expect sluggish, lie-around language. As for the active voice—zippy, good-time words. Even worse, what's with that "voice"? Follow this reasoning and you'd think you should reserve the passive voice for melancholy movies about things such as people dying from tuberculosis, and the active voice for James Bond flicks.

Through all this confusion, people concoct their own ideas about active and passive, and who can blame them? Some think you should write in the present tense only. Others think you should use short sentences. Still others think you should avoid helping verbs and sentences such as: "He was embezzling for 15 years," and say: "He embezzled for 15 years."

So let's set the record straight. Remember that sentence structure nugget we talked about in the chapters about nouns and verbs? We discussed that the order of noun and verb goes: noun–verb. Let's return to that idea, and to Todd and Trish, whom you met in Chapter 4. Here's what we had: "Todd organized the files." Basic, right? That's the active voice. Throw in an introductory element and you have:

> *When organizing the files, Todd confused Ted Patterson's file with Trish Hartley's.*

Who did the action? Todd. What did he do? He confused. What did he confuse? The files. It's all nice and tidy. That's the active voice. You can have lots of actors and actions in the sentence, of course—otherwise, how would you write those compound and compound–complex sentences we talked about earlier? Here's an example of the active voice with lots of actors and actions:

> *When organizing the warehouse purchase orders, Todd confused Ted Patterson's file with Trish Hartley's, so she received a note from the Hair Club for Men, who said they would deliver her order shortly.*

Yes, the active may seem basic, and it is. But people get off track in these four ways:

Passive #1: You separate the actor and the action in the sentence. You probably learned this standard "don't do" in high school English classes; the example they probably used was about someone and a door, like: "The door was closed by Trish." "Closed" comes first, Trish comes second. Should be the other way around. As in:

> *Trish closed the door.*

Here's another example:

> *Actually, hair-removal cream was ordered by Trish...*

should be:

> *Actually, Trish ordered hair-removal cream.*

Tighter, more direct. Just a better sentence.

Passive #2: No actor. That's it. None. This is the most common passive problem, and a real problem it is. Here's an example from the *real* Hair Club, formally known as the Hair Club for Men:

Hair Club exclusively provides only Follicular Unit Hair Transplantation, considered to be the gold standard of the industry.

Find the passive? They conveniently leave out *who* considers them the gold standard. Formerly bald people everywhere? The Gold Standard Committee on Hair Loss? Businesses love this handy little wording, since they can claim all sorts of things without attributing them to anyone in particular.

The wound only deepens with longer, often more complex, copy. The tone sounds stodgy, the sentence structure suffers, and the content? No one knows what you're talking about. Look at this example, also from the marketing folks at Hair Club:

Many grafts are destroyed or wasted without using the most modern hair transplant techniques in follicle extraction.

Get it? Neither did I. From what I *can* get, the grafts need to use the most modern hair transplant techniques with follicle extraction. Frankly, I didn't know grafts did follicle extraction. What they probably mean is:

When transplant technicians [or whatever they're called] don't use the most modern hair transplant techniques, they destroy or waste grafts in follicle extraction.

Passive #3: Not your traditional passive, this is the drag queen of word use. Some people call it a "hidden verb" because the verb pretends to be a noun. You can often (but not always) recognize these babies by the telltale "-ment" or "-tion" at the end. For example, our friends at the Hair Club call what they do "follicle extraction." Here, "extraction" looks like a noun but is really the verb "to extract." What are they extracting, exactly? Follicles would make sense, but can you actually *extract* follicles? Besides, who's extracting them? The folks over at Hair Club? Hair Club Extraction specialists? Hair Club extraction consultants? Are these guys doctors? Are they licensed? What?

The people who concoct these pseudo-words are especially fond of using them in names, as in the Hair Club's Follicular Unit Hair Transplantation that we mentioned earlier. We don't actually know what this particular event entails—a transplantation procedure? A transplantation gel? What we do know is it's the gold standard of the industry, and thanks to the hidden verbs, makes absolutely no sense.

Lest you think I'm picking on the Hair Club, let's look at some hidden verbs in the women's look-good world:

◆ Liz Arden. They offer a special lipstick, actually a lip *treatment*, called the Eight-Hour Lip Protectant Stick Sheer Tint SPF 15. The hidden verb is the "protectant." What exactly is a "protectant," you may ask? I asked that too.

◆ Neutrogena. Same product, but the name makes not a shred more sense. Doesn't matter; the hidden verb is there, making the whole thing look official: Lip Nutrition Soothing Mint Balm.

◆ Revlon. Same product, only they describe it as "Moisturous" and promise "100 percent instant moisturization." Moisturization. Even my spell checker doesn't have it.

It's not just marketers—everyone uses these hidden verbs—in proposals, news releases, Web pages. Aside from sounding bloated and pretentious, hidden verbs fail in another way. Because they're verbs pretending to be nouns, the sentence often omits who is doing the action *and* who is receiving it. Does this look familiar?

An immediate execution of key personnel in client sites is a requirement.

Sounds like they're planning to kill the personnel, doesn't it? Anyway, who is executing and who is requiring? How's this for a better alternative:

We need to send key personnel to the client sites immediately.

Or how about this sentence?

Acknowledgement of employee contributions and interaction will help in the development of professional skills.

Catch those hidden verbs? They're "acknowledgement," "inter-action," and "development." The rewrite, complete with actors and objects, would look a whole lot saner:

> *By interacting with employees and acknowledging their contributions, you'll help them develop professional skills.*

Of course, if you want to go lowbrow, just say:

> *You better pay more attention to the employees. They have no idea what they're doing.*

You may be wondering why "contribution," with its suspicious looking "-tion" at the end, isn't a hidden verb. Because, in this sentence it really functions as a noun, which, I know, makes the whole matter more confusing. Think of it this way: If hidden verbs are drag queen words, with the verb dressed up as a noun, then a word like "contribution" is like a female drag queen—a noun disguised as a verb impersonating a noun. Did that help?

Passive #4: In the pecking order of problem passives, consider this one an afterthought: when you use "there are" and "it is" in a sentence—but the "there" and "it" don't actually represent anything; they're as unsubstantial as a hefty portion of cotton candy in your meal. Let's explore this problem, staying with our moist-lip theme for one more minute:

> *It is unlikely that the moisturous lip gloss will give the appearance of spit or grease coating the lips.*

> *There have been questions about how the Lip Nutrition Soothing Mint Balm can provide 'nutrition' to lips whose surface consists of cells that are dead.*

Notice that the first example opens with "it"—usually a pronoun. But if this "it" is a pronoun, what does it represent? *What* is unlikely? Same thing for "there." What have been the questions? The questions can't be themselves, right? The problem with these little devils isn't that the reader won't understand the meaning—it's obvious. But the passive creates wordiness and a meandering quality that's deadly for your message.

Anyway, here are the rewrites:

The moisturous lip gloss probably will not give the appearance of spit or grease coating the lips.

Women everywhere have asked how the Lip Nutrition Soothing Mint Balm can provide 'nutrition' to lips whose surface consists of cells that are dead.

Cousin It

We have two "its" in the same family, but they're cousins. Use one—don't use the other.

Don't use it: "It is a beautiful ship..." What is a beautiful ship? The "it" is an imposter, standing for nothing. Try: "The ship is beautiful."

Do use it: "It is big enough to fill the population of Manhattan." The "it" represents the ship. It works.

Q&P Break: On the Couch

The "Will," "Has Been," and "Are" Phobia: People know that one tip-off of the passive voice lies in those unsightly helping verbs that litter the page. So you may have a sentence such as: "Wigs and rags are considered one alternative to hair transplants. Once a strong wind blows, though, they are known to blow off the head." Spot the passive there? If not, turn on your helping verb sensor—that should do it. In this case, the helping verb is "are," which you find in "are considered" and "are known." You can rewrite in countless ways—one option would be: "Our clients considered wigs and rags as an alternative to hair transplants. Once a strong wind blew, though, the wigs blew off their heads."

Only one problem with the helping verb sensor— you must shut it off at the appropriate time.

Otherwise you'll develop unhealthy helping-verb-phobia. Afflicted people see a helping verb and BAM—they delete it from the page—similar to someone with arachnophobia stomping out a spider. Out damn passive! Sadly, they're killing off otherwise healthy sentences that actually rely on helping verbs to survive.

Are you helping-verb-phobic? See if you can distinguish whether these sentences are passive or active:

1. *Hair loss treatment ads have been the nemesis of the serious hair specialist.* (Active)

2. *The doctors had been railing against the ads, when they were distracted by an odd smell.* (Both)
   Active: *The doctors had been discussing the ads*
   Passive: *when they were distracted by an odd smell.*

3. *A bottle of hair gel had been left near the heater and a small fire was set.* (Passive)

And the Prize Goes to...

Put these passives together, and you'll have such unsightly written specimens as this one from a federal government Website introducing regulations. Strangely, it reads like a dream compared to the regulations themselves:

The Code of Federal Regulations (CFR) is the codification of the general and permanent rules published in the Federal Register by the executive departments and agencies of the Federal Government. It is divided into 50 titles that represent broad areas subject to Federal regulation. Each volume of the CFR is updated once each calendar year and is issued on a quarterly basis.

Passive batting average: About 95 percent.

Passive—Active Q&A

Q. Are you saying I should eliminate all passives, no matter what?

A. Absolutely not. I use passives in this book from time to time. Use them when they suit you—but only when the style helps convey your message—not because you can't figure out the active alternative. Whatever else, don't use the passive voice too much.

Q. How much is too much?

A. Depends who you ask. As usual, everyone has an opinion, and it's usually different from everyone else's. Some guidelines say limit the passive to 5 percent. Others say 10 percent. I think you should limit it to 3 percent, but I'd never admit that publicly or someone would accuse me of being a Grammar Maven.

Q. What if no one is doing the action? Shouldn't I use the passive voice then?

A. Things don't just happen—someone or something has to make them happen, right?

Q. Okay—then what if I don't want to say who's doing the action?

A. Lots of people do try to look good—or anyway, get out of looking bad—by using the passive. For example, who wants to admit they'll penalize a customer for late payments when they're closing a deal? They want to seem like good guys, right? So they use mangled sentences, which, by the way, fool no one, like: "A penalty will be applied if payments are not received on time." No one actually applies these penalties, or for that matter, receives them. Money is just an ugly detail no one wants to address.

The answer lies in tone, which we'll discuss later. For now, look at these examples:

Bad tone = Bad active: "You better pay up, and on time, or we'll heap on penalties that will make your hair curl."

Good tone = Good active: "Please send your payment on time so you can avoid paying penalties."

Q&P Break: Noun–Verb Again

You have to try this—I mean it. It's a three-step process, but it won't take long, and it will cure your passive problem. I've used it on the most hopeless cases and they've found quick success!

Step #1: Find your writing coaches or some other language aficionados and have them check for passives. Or check yourself, using the information here.

Step #2: If you're active—or at least active most of the time—skip the rest. If you're passive, see Step #3.

Step #3: Have a beer. Relax. Those other guys are off reading the next chapter: They don't know *you're* really the lucky one! Take some time and chill. Then, every time you write, use a noun (or pronoun)–verb–noun relationship. Sure, you can throw in a glue word or a preposition now and then, but basically: noun–verb–noun, and go heavy on the simple sentences. As in:

"I like a cool glass of beer."

Once you have the active voice nailed—usually within a few hours—then use the sentence variety we discussed earlier. Just make sure you—not the sentences—have control, and you can turn on the active voice when you most need it.

And Now...A Few Words on Being Concise

Concise word use ranks high in the plain language priority list. Too high a word use per content ratio and the language flattens. The reader gets bored. The message languishes unread. Let's break the wordiness problem into four telltale types. Naturally, you should check for these problems in your own writing, with a little help from your friends.

Wordiness Problem #1: Small-Word Buildup

Of all the writing problems in the world, I'd rather have this one. Small-word buildup is easy to see, easy to fix, and easy to avoid. Basically, the extra words build up on the page similar to layers of oil in a pan. After a while, you're left with sludge. Spotting the problem is delightfully easy—just think size, as you can see in this (fictitious) example from BioTechnical Conglomerates, International:

> *It is important for us to consider as an integral part of this ad campaign that you project an image of BioTechnical Conglomerates, International in a manner that is clear and that everyone who needs to receive it can understand. This includes, but is not limited to, the public, shareholders, and Congress. These days, life seems complicated and difficult, unlike the past when horses and buggies were the norm and life was simpler. That is why it is also critical that we position our efforts to clone everything from individual human beings to the entire communities in which they live as something that results not from modern science, per se, but from old-fashioned community and family values. It is also important, as a result of this, that they see cloning as American as apple pie.*

You don't have to dig for the small-word buildup—you don't even have to *read*—just look:

> *It is important for us to*
> *as a... of this... that you...*
> *in a manner that is*
> *who needs to receive it*
> *This includes, but is not limited to,*
> *That is why it is also*

*in which they live as something that results not from... but from
It is also important, as a result of this, that they...*

Once you spot the words, cut them out and tidy up the remaining sentences. So here's the rewrite:

We must consider an integral part of this ad campaign a clear message about BioTechnical Conglomerates, International that everyone can understand. This includes, but is not limited to, the public, its shareholders, and Congress. These days, life seems complicated and difficult, unlike the past when horses and buggies were the norm and life was simpler. We must also position our efforts to clone everything from individual human beings to entire communities as something that results not from modern science, per se, but from old-fashioned community and family values. Then, they will see cloning as American as apple pie.

Okay, it's not great—but that's because I crammed just about every kind of wordiness problem into this one example that I could. But you must admit, it sounds better. Here are some other examples:

With small-word buildup: *In order to convince the public, who is skeptical to begin with, that cloning lots of people at one time is not a bad idea, we must be sure to have a homegrown, Mama-and-apple-pie approach.*

Concise and clean: *To convince a skeptical public that mass cloning is a good idea, we need a homegrown, Mama-and-apple-pie approach.*

With small-word buildup: *Should this campaign somehow lead to a Congressional hearing, it is incumbent on our ad committee to be willing to switch directions and immediately address the new set of issues.*

Concise and clean: *Should this campaign spark a Congressional hearing, our ad committee must immediately address the new issues.*

Suffering from Passive Pain?

The passive voice, our nemesis from the last section, brings on sometimes major bouts of wordiness. Look at the difference:

Passive: *The matter will be addressed by Congress and it will be viewed on the television by a large audience.*

Active: *Congress will address the matter and a large audience will watch it on the television.*

Wordiness Problem #2: Repeats

Repeats: mischievous little demons that creep into writing. Sometimes you can see them—when a word appears over and over—and sometimes you can't. Sometimes the repeats underscore your point, like "sometimes" and "over" in this paragraph, and sometimes they don't. Usually the repeats sneak into copy most unceremoniously, disguised as something fresh and interesting. Let's do a double-take on the previous paragraph about the ad campaign for BioTechnical Conglomerates, International, and see if you can spot the repeats there:

> *We must consider an integral part of this ad campaign a clear message about BioTechnical Conglomerates, International that everyone can understand. This includes, but is not limited to, the public, its shareholders, and Congress. These days, life seems complicated and difficult, unlike the past when horses and buggies were the norm and life was simpler. We must position our efforts to clone everything from individual human beings to entire communities as something that results not from modern science, per se, but from old-fashioned community and family values. Then, they will see cloning as American as apple pie.*

Here they are:

Repeat #1: Pairings. In this case I am speaking of words numbers five and six: "integral part." If it's a part, it's integral, right? Ditto for combos such as "completely honest," "complete stop," "dollar amount," "sum total," and "final decision." If you want more examples, just check your average contract or financial statement.

Repeat #2: Repeats via educated ignorance. Educated professionals adore these words—especially lawyers. They insist on wordy phrases such as the one lodged in line two: "including, but not limited to." "Including" already implies "not limited to."

Repeat #3: Double descriptors. In which you describe one thing twice, maybe three times in a single, overburdened line. In this paragraph, the line presents itself early on with this: "... a clear message... that everyone can understand." If it's clear, everyone should understand it. What are the options?

Repeat #4: New, old information. If you spotted this one—good work: "old-fashioned community and family values," and "They will see cloning as American as apple pie." Actually, "American as apple pie" represents those old-fashioned community and family values, so why bother mentioning all three? Scrape away the repeats and you're left with this nugget:

This ad campaign should contain a clear message about BioTechnical Conglomerates, International to the public, its shareholders, and Congress. These days, life seems complicated and difficult, unlike the past when horses and buggies were the norm and life was simpler. We must position our efforts to clone everything from individual human beings to entire communities as something that results not from modern science but is as American as apple pie.

Okay, now we're moving, and life is looking sweet without those repeats...except for a few more problems. But they're not repeats. Here's what they are.

Q&P Break

This exercise is great therapy—kind of similar to cleaning your car or a feng shui makeover. Count the words in an obviously wordy paragraph. Then cut the small-word buildup and tidy up the paragraph a bit. Now count again to see how many words you dropped. And there it is: tangible evidence of your success.

Wordiness Problem #3: Obvious Information

Don't worry; I won't define "obvious information." That would be too ironic. The sad part, though, is that writers place obvious information in the beginning of otherwise perfectly good copy, such as marketing material. Thus, the reader is immediately treated to such ludicrously unscintillating points as: "Everyone likes to save money," which is true but so obvious, why mention it? Or how about: "Ever want to get away from it all?" What are the possible options there? "No thanks, I love all the demands and the stress of everyday life." And finally, this little beauty for antacids: "It's no fun getting gas." True—except if you're a 10-year-old boy, in which case the emissions can lead to curious antics.

You'll find a plethora of obvious information in proposals too—especially the ones that start out telling prospects something they already know about themselves, such as "The workplace can be full of hazards—and you, as an employer, must pay the bill." Uh-huh, so *that's* why we've been paying for those insurance policies all this time. Then there's the obvious information wedged into everything from e-mails to Websites that starts with: "As you probably know..."

Rule of thumb: if they probably know, don't say it. But if you must, say something *about* it instead.

By the way—did you spot the example of obvious information in the previous paragraph? It was in the line: "... unlike the past when horses and buggies were the norm and life was simpler." This line is actually a two-fer, suffering from Wordiness Problem #4, as well.

Wordiness Problem #4: Unnecessary Content

How many times have you witnessed this problem in contracts, letters from your insurance company, and marketing material you *can* live without? Those endless trails of unnecessary information that turn perfectly good one-line communications into dry-as-dirt diatribes. Sometimes they drag on for a few lines, just as the BioTech folks who added the horse-and-buggy line. Who cares about horses and buggies when you're talking about cloning entire communities? Delete it and nothing's lost but the filler.

Other times, the unnecessary content wears on for page after page. True, plenty of professionals will defend this black hole of information—but don't be fooled. You can cut with no evident disadvantage. Here are a few examples of when anxiety might overwhelm your ability to press the delete key:

Letters, responding to questions, and (most especially) complaints. You start the letter something like this:

This is in response to your letter dated March 25, which you wrote regarding your request for a refund for the hair curling set you purchased on March 1. In the letter you said all the parts were not in the package, and that you only received the curling iron, brush, and rollers…

Okay, the reader knows all this. She wrote the letter. You're wasting her time, your energy, and perfectly good paper. So mention her letter and move on. Here goes:

Regarding your March 25 inquiry, the hair curling set you purchased on March 1 only comes with a curling iron, brush, and rollers, not the gel or conditioner and shampoo set, as you thought. Those were on the box for demonstration purposes only—as indicated in the footnote in tiny yellow letters in the left corner of the box. You can purchase these items separately, though, for a complete salon experience at home.

Sorely tempted? Enclose a copy of her letter. It's a quick and easy alternative. If you're addressing more complex issues, with high lawsuit potential, keep reading.

Claims and other complex policy decisions. You feel compelled (perhaps encouraged by the legal department) to give a full summary of every transaction that occurred with the reader for the past 10 days or 10 years. So you go on and on with this history, which the reader knows, and you know, and by a page number possibly in the double digits, tell them your company's decision. Which is all they wanted to know, anyway. So cut the history and get to the point.

Sorely tempted? That's probably because all that history/filler isn't for the reader at all—it's for the reader's lawyer, should they decide to sue. So you have three choices. Best choice: offer to send the full support document if they want it. Plenty of my clients, with high lawsuit potential, chose this option. They shaved the time necessary to get the letter out from days to an hour, the customer was satisfied, if only because the most important point was immediately visible, and as for the legal protection—all was neat and tidy. That's Option #1.

Option #2: Cut the history down to the bare bones. Have an interaction? Don't quote pertinent parts, don't distill it, just reference the letter, phone call, whatever, and move on. You still have the history, which should satisfy everyone's lawyers, and you don't have to write a novel to make your point. Oh—be sure to mention you'll send the real deal if they want it.

Finally, Option #3: write the decision as a one-page letter; then enclose the support material as an attachment. The core information—your decision—will still be visible, right there for you to see. And if they're hungry for more, they can flip to the rear for support.

Proposals. Details about how you create a system, program, or process. Think: result. The reader wants results. What result will they get for your efforts? Granted, if you're a contractor remodeling someone's kitchen, you do need to enlighten them about how long you'll leave the stove disconnected. And yes, definitely get detailed about costs—people are touchy about money. Show them how much more efficient they'll be in their new kitchen, how much longer their food will keep, and how much more impressive it will look, and any other results they can't help but love.

Sorely tempted to mention the history anyway? Don't be tempted. This is marketing material. Give them the plan *after* you close the deal. But if you *must*—mention the big picture steps, no details, with the benefits for the reader listed first. We'll talk more in the next chapter on reader-focus.

Wordiness Problem #5: Overgeneralization

Problem #5 is a great grand finale for this section of the book and is prevalent in marketing material, proposals, job announcements, newsletters—just about any document in which you proclaim your greatness. Usually, the language goes something like this:

> *At Hair Curl, Incorporated we care about all our customers. That's why we tailor our services to your individual needs at all of our salons. If you're planning to go out when our beauty salons are closed and need a consultation, you can always go on our Website. It's available 24-7, every day of the year.*

The information is so general (and obvious, and loaded with tiresome little words) it basically says nothing. Extra words, extra filler. Think you're writing this kind of nonsense but aren't sure? Do this: Exchange your company name and your offering with someone else's. If it fits perfectly, you have a problem. Look:

At Tony's Oil and Grease we care about all our customers. That's why we tailor our services to your car's individual needs at all of our garages. If you're planning to go out when our garage is closed and need a consultation, you can always go on our Website. It's available 24-7, every day of the year.

See what I mean? But get those specifics in there, and the message is full of substance, no extra words, and all yours. Now look:

At Hair Curl, Incorporated we offer everything from wraps to permanents at our salons. Need a personalized consultation when our salons are closed? Get on our Website to learn about the best gels for the worst weather, the right way to turn a French twist, how many curlers is one too much, and plenty more!

As for Tony's Oil and Grease?

At Tony's Oil and Grease we offer everything from wraps to permanents at our salons...

Don't think so.

As for Cloning...

Here's the final product, distilled from BioTechnical Conglomerates, International's wordy sample from pages ago:

This ad campaign should convince the public, shareholders, and Congress that BioTechnical Conglomerates, International's efforts to clone individuals and entire communities is as American as apple pie.

The Style–Content Connection

Cutting wordiness feels so good, once you're in the groove, you just cut, cut, cut. It's like a cool drink on a hot afternoon. Ahhh... the relief. But watch for signs of addiction. That occurs when you start cutting and cutting—you can hardly help yourself. Then there you are, sucking out vital content or disturbing the tone, as one addict/manager did to the bouncy holiday notice his employee composed. It started this way:

> *Come to the Holiday Party this Friday, December 20 at 9:00 p.m., at The Trader Lounge, Bar 'n' Grill. Bring a friend and bring your dancing shoes and boogie down to Eddy the Jumpin' DJ's tunes.*

Sadly, the manager cut it into this dreary, albeit more concise, version:

> *The Holiday Party will be held this Friday, December 20 at 9:00 p.m., at The Trader Lounge, Bar 'n' Grill. Guests welcome. Dancing included.*

The moral of this story: cut the words you don't need—keep the words you do.

Chapter 9
Reader-Focus:
Bowing to the King and Queen of the Universe

Let's talk about reader-focus. It's probably the most overlooked aspect of business writing around, although some, like advertisers, have it nailed. Can't think of an example? Then think Nike. No question, their logo: "Just do it," speaks directly to you. They don't even bother telling you *what* to do—but who cares? With language like that they don't need to.

Reader-focus isn't a big deal, really. You use it all the time. For example, if you bumped into an old friend, the exchange may have gone this way:

You: Hey, Bob, how are you? I haven't seen you in ages.

Bob: Oh my God, is that you, Ted? How the hell are you? You look great. What have you been up to?

> **You:** Oh, I'm working at Hyperion—I'm the CIO. They're a great company and have a knockout marketing and ad campaign.
>
> **Bob:** Wow—never heard of them. Actually, I'm a stay-at-home-dad these days. So I don't hear about a whole lot besides Melba toast and diapers.
>
> **You:** No kidding. You like it?
>
> **Bob:** Sure do.

No question, you're talking to Bob, and he's talking to you. You call him "Bob." He calls you "Ted" and you call each other "you." Bob tells you about his life as a stay-at-home-dad, not about his toothache, his divorce 12 years ago, or his taste in music. You tell him about your great job at Hyperion. And both of you use words that make sense so you can understand each other.

Call it informal language, spoken communications, whatever. In essence, this conversation can be hailed as a great example of reader- (or in this case "listener-") focus. It's normal. It's natural. And it's logical. Which *doesn't* explain why people in the business world have such difficulty using it. So here's what you do:

There's No Writing but Marketing Writing

Many reader-focus concepts come straight from advertising and marketing. But, you may be thinking, I don't write marketing material. I write policy manuals for a health plan. Or I write safety manuals for an automobile parts manufacturer. Or I write e-mails. That's it. Just e-mails. Doesn't matter. Consider everything you write a marketing piece. You must market that policy. That procedure. That request you send across the virtual channels.

Pointer #1: Use *You*

Using the second person "you" in conversation is a sign that you're normal and not suffering from any psychological disconnects. Without the "you," you'd wind up with a conversation similar to this:

> **You:** Hey, person walking down the street, how is he? I haven't seen that person in ages.

Bob: Oh my God, is that a person who has been missing from my life for ages? How the hell is he? He looks great. What is that individual up to?

No doubt, you naturally gravitate to the second person in your e-mails. But the second person suits all messages: serious-as-death regulations, and lighthearted party invitations. Yet chances are, the more serious the topic, the more you deviate. Here's how:

Passive. It's back. Again. Look at the effect of the passive in this line from an e-mail:

Data about the relationship between cannibalism and community cloning is needed...

Who needs it? And worse, who should send it? The reader may never know. So rewrite in the second person:

Would you please send me data about the relationship between cannibalism and community cloning?

Consider yourself using the second person when you address the reader directly (the imperative voice), as in: "Please send me data."

Mass anonymity. Let's say you're giving advice on your Website about how to use an ATM. When writing to one person, albeit an unknown person, you might say something like:

If you lose your ATM card, call the bank immediately.

The "you" seems to slide in easy as a seed in watermelon. But when addressing customers en masse, suddenly, you start writing:

When customers withdraw money, they should protect their pin numbers from criminals who might be watching.

This switch has no logic. No purpose.

Uncertain volume. I've heard this one a lot when training—what if you're writing to one person, such as the ATM user, and lots of people, such as employers... all in one paragraph. How will the reader distinguish between the one-person "you" and the many-people "you," aka the singular and the plural? Yes, the inconsistencies of English really can be perplexing. The answer, in a nutshell, comes down to one word: transitions. So you'd write:

As employees, you owe it to your company to have personalized ATM cards with your company's logo in the left hand corner. If you don't have one, just call 1-800-ATM-COOL and we'll set you up.

The "you," thanks to ongoing inconsistencies in the English language, can apply to one person or many.

Think About This!

In this book, I'm using the second person consistently. Imagine if I wasn't? And I was referring to "you" as "the reader." Or "the person." And remember—I'm not writing to you alone (although you *are* my favorite reader). Lots of people are reading this book, and every one of them is "you."

Love From Afar?

The trick to strong writing is getting your readers to participate in, interact with, and *own* the message. If you speak directly to them, using "you," they're immediately engaged—the message is about *them.* Use the third person and speak generically about the "customer," or the "student" or the "employee," and your readers are outside the message, reading about someone else.

Pointer #2: Focus on them. Not you. Not your product. Not your needs.

This one is tough—even tougher than the second person, and involves writing from the reader's perspective, not your own. See how it plays out:

E-mail

Focus on you:

Sylvia, I need the PIN for the ATM card immediately as I need to get money for my airplane ticket for the conference in Rome.

Focus on reader:

Sylvia, if you want to see me in Rome next week, send me the PIN for the ATM card so I can get my airplane ticket.

Focus on you:

I need to receive the completed form B-FY2008 by noon tomorrow or I will not be able to address your funding requests.

Focus on reader:

If you want funding for this year, complete and send me form B FY2008 by noon tomorrow.

Marketing Material

Focus on you:

We're currently going through the completion stage of the process to make this new service available to all our customers. Among the benefits we're offering, we can put our customers' logos on their employees' ATM cards. It will enhance the company image to their employees.

Focus on reader:

Want your employees to really love you? Then take advantage of Banker's Best's new service: Get your company logo on their ATM card. They'll think of you fondly every time they open their wallet.

Inquiry Response to a Letter

Focus on you:

I have reviewed the question which you asked in your letter of May 19 and have sought information to provide a fair and honest answer. What I found was that while our business customers can get their logo on their ATM card, they cannot give customers the option of having photos of their pets or kids.

Focus on reader.

Your question, in your May 19 letter, as to whether employees can place pictures of their kids or pets on their ATM card, brings up a great idea! Perhaps someday the answer will be yes—for now your company logo must suffice.

Case Study

And the Award Goes To...

Some writers get the reader-focus. Look at this bit I found in an ad from *The New York Times* business section:

Technology drives innovation. That makes you the Chief Innovation Officer. So how do you transform innovation from a buzzword into a sustainable part of your business? Visionary CIOs are leading the way with Hyperion performance management solutions. With Hyperion, you break down the barriers between finance, operations, and planning, and align them around a master data set. You give everyone the tools they need to continuously analyze and manage business performance—and invent new ways to improve it. Isn't that what real innovation is all about?

Does the message speak to you, personally? Does it move and engage you? Not me either. But that's the point. This message isn't intended for you or me—unless you're a CIO. Then it's you and no one but you. As for Hyperion? They're just the helper.

Q&P Break on Reader-Focus: The Dilemma

So how do you create that all-important reader-focus in a newsletter? Announcement? In any document with an indirect connection to the reader? Think movie—think newspaper. Focus on the most exciting, unusual, or surprising points. If you're not sure what I mean, get a pile of magazines, from *Time* to health and fitness publications. And while you're at it, pick up your local newspaper. Journalists position their articles for maximum attention.

On the Couch

Okay, sit back, relax. Let's talk. You grew up writing essays that began: "In the following, I will discuss..." and writing about: "The person who means the most to me..." and "Why I like/dislike *The Scarlet Letter.*" You learned to place yourself and your thoughts at the center of the universe. Then you moved into the business world where you were taught to place your company in that center spot: your company's profits, your company's products, your company's commitment to meeting something—usually someone's needs. As for the reader? The customer? Huh?

Breaking that habit requires more than strong word use. It requires a reality shift. But don't worry, once you get the hang of it, reader-focus will flow easily. And the payoffs? They'll be big.

Pointer #3: Power Positioning

Consider your message an ad. It must be quick. Sharp. And gripping. All in the first three or four words, tops. Here are a few hints about how. We'll cover more later.

Hint #1: The first line is everything. That means your subject line, header, sub-header. Vanish the old subject lines that state: "Form B-FY2008 Due" and other energy-zappers. Opt for more energetic alternatives such as "Don't lose funding!" Or go for the "heart attack" type subject lines: "You Lost Your Funding..." Then in the message, immediately start with, "... if you don't send me Form B-FY2008 by noon tomorrow."

Hint #2: Put the most critical information in the *first* paragraph. Don't wander in. Don't lead. Don't set them up. Don't squander. Get that point right in there. Tell them what they must know—and motivate them to act. And make it interesting—use quotes, surprising numbers, anecdotes, whatever works.

Hint #3: You know those headers you use between sections of longer documents like reports, proposals, and manuals? Usually they're as compelling as dust and contain less substance. So before you write that header, try infusing it with energy. Here's how:

- ◆ **Inject a verb in there.** A typical header might read: "Background." Pretty noun-ish, which might be okay, but it's also a general noun, which, as you may remember, doesn't resonate.

So try for something energetic and compelling: "Historical Trends that Reveal Your Financial Future."

◆ **Give them information.** "Background" sits there. But "Historical Trends"? Who knew there were historical trends worth mentioning? Who knew they could help predict the future?

◆ Move the structure. So after you write, "Historical Trends that Predict Your Future," you tell what that future will bring. But which of these sounds better?

Next Steps

The Future: 10 Predictions of What's Ahead

Pointer #4: Show, Don't Tell

"Show, don't tell" ranks as one of the top priorities in fiction and journalism but whimpers or dies in the business world. Remember: the reader doesn't care about you. Doesn't care about your insights, your opinions, or even your experience, unless you happen to be Prince Charles, Oprah, or (for reasons we have yet to discover) Paris Hilton. Instead, your readers want to see the action for themselves. That's the difference between *showing* and *telling*. Look:

In fiction:

Tell: The actress Stella Carp was a beautiful woman.

Show: Stella Carp was voluptuous—at 5-foot 5-inches she weighed 160 pounds—every inch sumptuous curves and silken skin.

In advertising:

Tell: The actress Stella Carp gained an enormous amount of weight in a relatively short time. She needed a plan that worked fast so she could accept a role in an important film. That's why she picked us.

Show: Stella Carp gained 300 pounds in only two years. She needed a diet plan to drop it all within six months to star in *Cleopatra* with Tom Cruise. That's why she picked us.

In a doctor's report:

Tell: The actress Stella Carp suffers from a weight problem. This has affected various parts of her body and could affect others.

Show: Stella Carp suffers from clinical obesity. This has put enormous strain on her knees—she now needs a cane to walk—and puts her at high risk for Type 2 Diabetes.

Still not clear about the show and tell difference? Here's a quick cheat sheet:

The Not-So-Famous "Show, Don't Tell" Cheat Sheet

Telling	Showing
wealthy	richer than the Queen of England
smart	I.Q. of 190
busy	booked solid all week
fast	#1 in the state relay races
thick (as in book)	1976 pages!
thick (as in person)	I.Q. of 50
soon	in two minutes
tired	dragging
good	chocolatey
ancient (to a kid)	43 years old
young (to a senior)	43 years old

The "Show, Don't Count" Phenomenon

In their efforts to cut messages down to their skinny best, some people balk at the "showing" and not "telling" idea. The descriptions, numbers, and images make the message longer. So remember the concise golden rule: Cut the words you *don't* need. But you *do* need the ones that show.

A "Show, Don't Tell" How-To

What's the secret to showing? Nothing short of making a movie and letting the film roll. The reader must get a mental picture, and savor the sounds, smells, even feelings. But wait, you're thinking, how is this possible with business writing? With financial writing? With policy writing for heaven's sake, which is as flat and "unfeeling" as...policy writing? Here are seven tips for showing and not telling no matter what you write. Consider it notes for a film treatment.

Tip #1: Specifics. We talked about specifics; here's a reminder. The difference between "lots of weight" and "300 pounds" comes down to the difference between a general statement and a specific one. The specific statement lets the readers see for themselves. You gained weight, sure. But if you gained five pounds over the summer, the culprit is obviously that beer we mentioned earlier. Stop by the gym more often and forget about it. But 300 pounds?

Tip #2: Facts. And nothing but the facts. Well, except the source of the fact. Why do you think Stella can lose all that weight in six measly months? Because scientific studies say so. Then comes that other small matter: *What* scientific studies? At this point, many organizations get creative and say things such as: "Researchers in our lab found that you, like Stella, can lose over 100 pounds and three inches in six measly months—*without* giving up the food you love!" You've got to love them...and the researchers. In the TV ads, they usually flash on some guy in a white robe, possibly the company computer geek. No matter—they never said their researcher had a Ph.D.; was associated with, say, a hospital; or actually did *medical* research.

True, some organizations have their own research institutes, or the funds to finance a study elsewhere. Then the results may be miraculous. Dubious, but miraculous. The food industry engages in this practice shamelessly. They dig up scientists with such brain-numbing findings as "chocolate is good for your teeth," which entitles them to say: "As part of Stella's healthy diet, she eats at least one full-size chocolate bar a day."

Don't make up sources. It's obvious and unnecessary. Oh, and illegal. Did I mention illegal?

Tip #3: Numbers, percents, degrees. I don't know about you, but I love a good number. I've dabbled in quite a few here, such as the first three or four words that matter most in a message. If you're prone to numbers overload, though, beware. Too many tucked in a paragraph and your reader's eyes glaze over. Even worse, they think the writer is showing off. But if you're writing an annual report or other number-dependent piece, what should you do? Think charts, baby. Think charts, graphs, and other visual enhancements, and leave the narratives for actual words.

Tip #4: Names. Drop them. Shamelessly. People love names. They give your writing authority and can wiggle into your copy in countless ways. There's the old quote-at-the-beginning idea—favorites include JFK, Roosevelt, and Albert Einstein. Or wiggle them into your text by, for example, saying that: "This diet is based on Atkins' concept that any carb is one too many..."

Tip #5: Use those powerful strategies known as The Testimony. Most commonly associated with ads for diet plans—you know the bit: "This is me last summer when I weighed 300 pounds. Now this is me at a mere 160." Plenty of ads clinch the deal with before-and-after pictures—usually involving swimsuits.

Testimonies work wonders in job announcements that quote employees saying how much they love their jobs; in reports in which witnesses or experts discuss otherwise dubious views; and in Web pages, which often contain pictures and voice-overs. A few closing points about this idea:

◆ Sure you can say it yourself. But who's going to believe *you*? Would you really speak ill of your own product? I mean, would the makers of a diet plan ever say: "Our plan is so bad, even our healthy customers end up with anemia or acute diabetes"? But if a happy customer lost weight almost overnight? Then it's *got* to be true. HHaving By the way—the reliability quota rises for some reason if that someone has a famous name, Ph.D., great figure, or lots of money.

◆ Name your expert. A line such as: "I think the CEO stinks," is better left anonymous, but give that happy employee who says "This is the best place I've ever worked; I love it here!" a name and title. Full names work best, but even "Carole, Receptionist" is better than a nameless smiling face.

◆ If using a quote, make sure it sounds as if someone actually said it. Use relaxed words and snappy, albeit appropriate, expressions. Quoting a CEO? Don't use "stink," as in, "The employees here stink," but something similar to "are ineffective." On the other hand, avoid industry garble, such as: "The employees have a deficit of skills naturally acquired through experiential and pedagogically programmed knowledge."

◆ Don't drop names of unpopular people. Richard Nixon: out. Bill Clinton: in, unless you're writing to a Republican campaign committee. But then, Richard Nixon would *still* be out and George W., iffy.

By the way, avoid quotes attributed to nonexistent or unknown entities, such as "a wise man" or "one famous leader" or "according to someone." They miss the point.

Tip #6: Describe. Now we're back to specifics. Take 300 pounds. You create an image the reader can see. This activates at least one sense, their vision, and deepens their involvement in their message. The more intense—and unique—the image, the better.

No image: She got heavier.

Image: She ballooned out.

The reader sees the image of a balloon getting bigger and bigger, and gets a sense of tension as the air presses against the sides. But remember: Keep the image fresh. Clichés or tired expressions reign as verbal valium for even the most scintillating messages. Take: "He's thick as a brick." Who envisions a guy with a brick for a brain? Same thing with, "You can't run from the truth." You don't actually *see* someone running, right? Although, if you said, "You can't prance away from the truth," the reader would get an image of *something*. More about clichés in a minute.

Tip #7: Let's talk about metaphor again. You can build metaphor right into the sentence, as you saw with our description of Stella. A "difficult problem" becomes a "puzzle," an "enigma," a "brain twister," or a "mind-bender." Or you can use the "like" or "as" metaphors made famous in high school English classes everywhere, as in:

Losing weight can be like running up a steep mountain with cement boots on.

Or:

Every time Stella tried, she was as reasonable as a wild cat.

Or:

When she wore that red dress in Cleopatra she looked like a ripe strawberry.

Sure metaphors sound unique. And sure, they liven up the language. But they also enrich the reader's experience by playing off numerous senses—you can feel the weight of cement boots and imagine the sounds of a wild cat. As for connotations, "cement boots" have a definite Mafia quality to them. If you don't know what I mean, read *The Godfather*.

Here's another example:

No Metaphor: "That project is really important but we need to improve it."

Metaphor: "That project is like a blood-line to the client. At this point, we need a transfusion."

As for gratuitous metaphors? Use them if you can get away with it. Otherwise, better not.

Tip #8: Keep it fresh. Anything stale, dry, or dusty (those are metaphors, by the way; words can't really be any of those things) and you lose the reader's attention immediately. They're gone. Not interested. So long. To engage, delight, or—if you must—depress them, use unique alternatives and avoid these mind-numbers:

Clichés. Here we are again, discussing boring, flat, silly, and ineffective clichés. There's a bountiful variety in the business world. Go on *www.gardendigest.com*, and you'll find a list of clichés based on *gardens* alone. Here's a sample of what they cover:

Against the grain.

Al fresco.

American as apple pie.

Am I talking to a brick wall?

An apple a day keeps the doctor away.

An apple never falls far from the tree.

An axe to grind.

Ants in his pants.

The apple of his eye .

As clear as mud.

As cold as ice.

As common as dirt.

As delicate as a flower.

As fresh as a daisy.

Ashes to ashes, dust to dust.

As pure as snow.

As solid as the ground we stand on.

At the bottom of the pecking order.

At the crack of dawn.

I'm sure you could add a few dozen to the list. There are "plenty to go around."

Tired expressions. Tired expressions are the same as clichés, only less colorful. You sink into these deadeners with lackluster lines and with words like "convenience," as in: "We're at convenient locations," and, "We're open until 10:00 for your convenience," and that non-apology, "We're sorry for the inconvenience."

You could add to the list such loathsome lines as "Thank you in advance," and, "We appreciate your cooperation," so overused they're worse than meaningless—they're insincere. Here are a few more: "We are committed to getting this done in time," "We want to address all your needs," "Our customer is priority #1," "If you need us, just call," "We are always there for our employees," and, "We do the best that we can."

Q&P Break: Tell All

Speaking of "plenty to go around," draft a few common clichés and tired expressions. Then, every time you write, look for more, pull them, and add more interesting alternatives instead. Pass the list around, and send some to me and I'll post on the Web: *www.quickandpainlessbusinesswriting.com.*

Hold On! What Do I Do Instead?

Clichés may seem like the only option, but they're not. They are an option to avoid and are easy to replace. Just think up more specific alternatives. Own a restaurant that's open until 12:00 for your customer's "convenience"? Dump "convenience" and try something about keeping the doors open and lights burning so your customer can have a "midnight snack." Is your customer really your #1 priority? Then you must be a nonprofit organization. Otherwise, money comes first or you'll go out of business. So avoid the false line and show them how much you care with those fabulous brands, low prices, free delivery, and other perks.

Wait—We Weren't Done! Back to the Couch

Why So General...So Cliché...So Nonspecific?
Glad you asked. It bubbles up from three sources.
Source #1: Miss Ferguson and all the Miss Fergusons who taught everything from science to early American history. It went similar to this: Every time you wrote, you got grades. In fact,

probably the only time you *didn't* get grades was in creative writing class, where your teacher was too sensitive to bother. But you only got partial credit for that class, so it didn't really count.

So there you were, writing, and you weren't sure if 30 people or 300 people came over on the Mayflower, so you wrote: "Lots of brave pilgrims came over on the Mayflower." And voilà, you got a good grade. This happened over and over again until you developed a general jones, or to say it more clinically, an addiction to generic word use.

Source #2: The review process is the culprit at work. Who exactly is reviewing you? Your boss, coworker, or series of bosses—who cares? The less specific you are, the less can be criticized.

Source #3: Time. Well, that's what you think anyway, but it's not true. Clear, specific words are no harder to write than general ones. And if you're cutting and pasting paragraphs used in the past, then cut and paste specifics, too.

When Your Point of View Counts

Your point of view counts when you

◆ are an expert and everyone craves your opinion;

◆ experienced some unusual situation like a tidal wave and you've risen from the watery depths to tell us all about it;

◆ accomplished some great feat like losing 300 pounds in six months;

◆ are responding to something someone said about you;

◆ are giving your view based on personal knowledge of a situation.

Q&P: Tell ALL!

Please, please send your favorite quotes, clichés, and metaphors. I'd love to see them—and if they're good, I'll post!
www.quickandpainlessbusinesswriting.com

Chapter 10
The Truth About Tone, Damn It!

So I said to you:

Shut up. I'm so sick of hearing this garbage over and over...

No, wait. No I didn't. I said:

Let's not discuss this any more. We've already been through it before.

Actually, what I said was this:

Hey, cool it. Let's not go there again, okay?

Or did I? Maybe I was being diplomatic, humble, and sensitive, and so I said:

I see your point, and thanks for expressing it. Give me some time to think about it.

That is the idea of tone. Tone, like reader-focus, ranks high among the factors that determine how your reader responds to your message. Only hardly anyone knows that—especially in business writing. Even Websites, those carriers of speed, energy, and electricity; and e-mails, renowned for their informality, sometimes have all the tone of a medicine bottle.

We'll take a look at the Big Three of business writing tone—but first, a look at a tone wrecker: jargon.

All About Jargon!

Jargon ignites more controversy than Hillary Clinton, although I'm not sure why. It's unnecessary and ridiculous; the pestilence of business and academic writing. People who use it are showing off and should forget jargon and go to therapy instead. Add that other unappealing presence, industry terminology, and you get copy such as this:

Auxiliary verbs are conjugated depending on the subject of a sentence. Knowing the correct auxiliary verb usage is key to tense usage. Every tense takes an auxiliary form of the verb. There are three exceptions to this rule: Simple present positive: she works at a bank; simple past positive: he bought a new TV last week; and positive imperative statement: hurry up!

Sadly, I found this example on *esl.about.com*, written for those poor fools who want to learn English. What better way to teach them than to use English even native speakers can't understand?

Let's start with a definition of jargon, shall we? The Website MBA Jargon Watch (*www.johnsmurf.com/jargon*) defines jargon this way:

jargon \Jar"gon\, n. [F. jargon, OF. also gargon, perh. akin to E. garrulous, or gargle.] The specialized or technical language of a trade, profession, or similar group. Speech or writing having unusual or pretentious vocabulary, convoluted phrasing, and vague meaning.

Of course, you don't want to clump all alien words under the heading "jargon." Then you get into a tangle about who understands what and the whole problem festers even more than usual. Instead, break these words into two distinct categories: jargon and industry terminology.

Category 1: Jargon

Qualities:

◆ Specific to an industry or field: these are words you find nowhere else.

◆ Not in a grammatically correct style: much jargon contains hidden verbs, for example.

◆ Can be replaced with other words.

When to use: Never. The reader has no way of decoding the word. Follow typical language patterns instead. Besides, if you can replace the word with something clearer, why wouldn't you?

Let's look at this example:

Knowing the correct auxiliary verb usage is key to tense usage. Every tense takes an auxiliary form of the verb.

Okay, so let's get this straight. The "auxiliary verb usage" means what exactly? And how is that "usage" different from the "tense usage" and what is the difference between "auxiliary verb usage" and an "auxiliary form of the verb"? Presumably, if this example was in a book about English grammar, terms such as "auxiliary verb usage" would have been defined earlier in the book, and they would be fine to use. But if something similar to this is given as an answer to a simple question with no context, the jargon only confuses rather than clarifies.

Category 2: Industry Terminology

Qualities:

◆ Specific to an industry or field: these are words you find nowhere else.

◆ In a grammatically correct style.

◆ Cannot be replaced with other words.

When to use: When you have industry terminology you *know* you can't replace *and* works grammatically, you have three choices:

Choice #1: Use freely when the person understands the word. Don't be overconfident, though. Experts think they understand words they really don't. For example, I went to a conference once on something they called "complexity." At the end, after three days of mind-numbing conversation on the subject, someone asked: "But what do we mean by 'complexity' anyway?" Everyone in the three-day interchange had their own definitions of the subject at hand.

Choice #2: If you have a mixed insider–outsider audience, define the word for them. We're not talking glossary here; we're talking a few defining words built into the sentence. For example, some of my financial institution clients write to people about "lump sums" and "annuities." Naturally, you'd imagine everyone knows the difference between the two terms, but they don't—especially elderly farmers in the Midwest, whose Washington-speak is limited to what they learn from *The West Wing*. So you need to educate them with a gentle definition, such as:

> *If you want small payments every month in an annuity, check here_____.*

> *If you want to receive all your money at one time in a lump sum, check here_____.*

Or you could say:

> *Check here if you want an annuity in which you get small payments every month_____.*

> *Check here if you want a lump sum, which means you receive all your money at one time_____.*

Choice #3: If you have a mixed audience and you're only going to use the word once, forget the word and use the definition instead. There's no reason to introduce an alien term they'll never confront again.

On Closer Inspection: The Jargon–Industry Terminology Distinction

Both industry terminology *and* jargon relate to matters specific to your field. You wouldn't, for example, come home and say:

Oh, my darling auxiliary, such a tantalizing usage you have tonight.

And you certainly wouldn't want to raise issues concerning "tense usage" or "auxiliary usage."

But from there, the two categories part ways. Industry words make sense grammatically, even though few people understand them. And they have such specific meanings, you cannot replace them with alternatives. Take names, for example. Most industries have names for their products, methods, and tools that only they understand. Still, a name is a name. And if they say the "BioFornica Analysis Comprehension," provided interesting data, who are we to insist they rename...whatever it is.

By the Way, Have You Seen..? #1

If business writing or the business world gets you down, go to the Web site I mentioned earlier: *www.johnsmurf.com/jargon.* The site contains hilarious and revealing definitions of business jargon.

By the Way, Have You Seen..? #2

Check out this from the *Chronicle of Higher Education*—what they call their Information Technology Jargon Monitor: *http://chronicle.com/free/ it/jargon.htm*. They give you dirt on the latest terminology. Here's a peek:

Applehead *n.* A professor, student, or administrator who believes the Apple Macintosh to be the only viable personal computer.

back-seat mouser *n.* An overly helpful onlooker who constantly gives directions about where to point, click, and scroll.

bar-code hairstyle *n.* A term used by Japanese students (who say *"baakodo haasutyru"*) to describe male professors with thinning hair who comb what little they have left over their bald spots.

chalk and talk *n.* Derogatory term used to describe the traditional model of classroom instruction, in which a professor delivers a monologue, punctuated by chalkboard scrawling, before a passive group of students.

clicks and borders *n.* A new concern for college leaders, who now must worry not only about the traditional campus infrastructure—the bricks and mortar—but also the digital formatting and design elements of Websites that help define an institution's image in the public mind.

computer butt *n.* The unpleasant sensation that develops when one spends too much time sitting in front of a computer in an uncomfortable chair.

The Industry Terminology–Jargon Trail

A Case Study

Let's get back to that elderly farmer in the Midwest. I'm bringing him up, not because I think Midwesterners are naïve, but because he's real. As I recall, he was a Korean War veteran and was inquiring about his pension benefits and whether to include or omit his time fighting overseas in the years he worked. That calculation factored into the amount of his pension, which matters a lot, especially if you're on a fixed income.

My client sent the poor guy what they call an "Initial Determination Letter" at some point along the way, telling him their "initial determination." Several correspondences transpired, in which the Customer Service Representative cited the "Initial Determination Letter," which made as much sense to the guy as hip-hop. Here's why:

1. "Determination" doesn't tell who's determining what and falls under the dubious header of "hidden verb."

2. "Initial Determination." How can a "determination" be initial? Isn't that something you do at the *end* of the process? Doesn't initial mean "first of many?"

3. *What* initial determination letter? The guy got lots of letters lots of times, but none of them said "This is your initial determination letter," or had the words "NOTICE: Initial Determination Letter" or any other thing stamped on the front. It was just one of many letters.

So how do we address this matter? Is this disarming term industry terminology or jargon? Let's use our criteria to find out.

Criteria #1: Is it an industry term? Okay, that one's obvious. Who uses the term in real life? Can't you just see it?

Dear Bob, I sent you an Initial Determination Letter yesterday, responding to your inquiry of Saturday night, in which you requested to have fornication and other acts of substantial interest to you. In the above referenced e-mail, I mentioned that I gave the matter consideration, but upon review of the facts, i.e. your looks, personality, et al, the response was no. So please cease and desist from calling.

Criteria #2. Does it work grammatically? The answer, sadly, is yes. That's the name—unfortunate as the choice might be—of the letter. So yes, it *is* a viable, albeit undesirable, industry term and not jargon.

Criteria #3. Can you replace it with another word? Nope. A name is a name, as irreplaceable as the person or thing that bears it—unless the organization decided to change it.

So what to do, what to do? The option is actually easy: define it with a simple explanation, as in:

The Initial Determination Letter, which we sent you on March 14...

or some variation on that theme.

But the plot thickens, as it usually does in these matters, and perfectly fine (albeit distasteful) industry terminology morphs into jargon, wiggling its way into other parts of the text. In the letter, for example, the employees wrote about their "initial determination," as in: "The initial determination found that..."

How can a determination find anything? No, this makes no sense. Only now, "initial determination" is *jargon* because it

1. is no longer irreplaceable, since it's not the Name of the Thing, but just awkward wording;

2. is not grammatically correct—or shouldn't be, anyway;

3. can be changed without losing the meaning.

Here's the rewrite:

Our decision, which we discussed in our letter dated March 14, stated that...

Q&P Break

Keep a list of problem words at work—which ones are jargon? Which ones are industry terms? Then, create your own jargon–industry terms dictionary. Pass it on to your attorneys for their approval, and then they'll pass it on to everyone else. I've developed jargon dictionaries for lots of clients—including the Social Security Administration, a true jargon-holic—and it really helped!

Q&P Tell-All

You *must* send some of your worst-case jargon examples. Be sure to say which organization uses it—although we'll keep the name confidential if we post: *www.quickandpainlessbusinesswriting.com.*

Tone—The Big Three (Plus One Cousin)

Generally, tone squeezes into three forms: hyper-formal, formal, and informal. As for that cousin you saw in the header: meet the conversational tone, as in, "Hey man, good to see ya…" now a standard in business writing thanks to e-mails, blogs, and those bizarre little creatures: Blackberries. Here goes:

Hyper-formal
Qualities: Lots of jargon; lots of industry terminology; mangled usage; tired expressions, legal and otherwise; no resemblance to your usual written or spoken words.
Where you find it: Policy-based documents, academic publications,"experts" trying to appear smart.

How it reads: The determination as to above stated account indicates an underpayment of $450 per reg. FT675 due for remittance of payments to recoup that amount in the sum of $6 per pay period.

When to use it: Never.

Formal

Qualities: No jargon; some industry terms; common usage; distant, yet mildly approachable tone.

Where you find it: Some newspaper articles (in the business section), speeches, manuals, annual reports, job announcements, not-so-good Websites.

How it reads: We determined that we paid you $450 more than you were entitled to receive, according to reg. FT675. We will deduct $6 from your checks each month until we recoup that amount.

When to use it: Sometimes.

Informal

Qualities: No jargon, no industry terms, relaxed usage, approachable tone, varied sentence structure, mm-mm good.

Where you find it: Most mainstream newspapers and magazines, online and otherwise; newsletters; invitations; most e-mails; good Websites; most marketing material and ads.

How it reads: We discovered that we paid you too much money—$450, according to our regulations. But don't worry: We'll only deduct $6 from your monthly checks until we get that amount back.

When to use it: As often as possible, which is more often than you think.

Cousin Conversation

Qualities: Yup—jargon is back—only now as hip phrases, especially regarding technology. As for common usage, Why bother? Break the rules if it makes your message fun and approachable.

Where you find it: The virtual world; occasional newspapers and magazines; definitely e-zines, although these aren't exactly business writing documents; and occasional marketing material and ads.

How it reads: Sorry—our lawyers tell us we sent you way too much money—actually $450. Be cool: You won't feel strapped. We'll just take $6 every month from your check until we get it back. Hey—you won't even feel it.

When to use it: Occasionally, as your audience and genre allows.

The Audience Factor

You've probably heard you should vary your writing style for different audiences. One for the boss. One for coworkers. One for the client. That's true—and false. Generally, people appreciate relaxed, low-jargon, high-energy words. But rely on common sense—you might start an e-mail to a peer with "Hey, Stu—" but not an e-mail to a new client. Have questions? Think about how you'd address your reader in a face-to-face meeting.

Tone Reminder

Want a more relaxed tone? Have a piece that begs to be catchy, not formal and stiff, but the powers that be make that famous claim: "We have to write it this way!"? Remember, please: You don't have to write in a particular way.

Other Tones Too

Excited:

The temperature dropped in the lab! All the fruit flies are dead! Dr. Benson has to start all over again!

What it takes: Short sentences, quick rhythms, hard-sounding words.

Sensitive:

Dr. Benson must labor over the experiment yet again since all the fruit flies died when the temperature in the lab dropped.

What it takes: Longer sentences, softer verbs, more feeling-oriented content.

Serious:

Dr. Benson must duplicate the previous experiment since the original fruit flies died due to a temperature drop in the lab.

What it takes: Formal tone, longer sentences, words detached from emotional connotation.

Humorous:

The fruit flies froze to death, so Dr. Benson has to start all over again. They looked like mini-popsicles in the petri dish.

What it takes: Uneven sentence rhythms, informal tone, and an element of surprise, particularly at the end.

Q&P Break: Tone Hint

To create the right tone, use one part sentence structure, one part word use, and three parts intuition. To help your intuition along, try hearing the sentence in your head. Or try reading copy that's in the tone you want. As for an exercise—here are two, if you have a little time:

Exercise #1: Take a few samples from different genres: your e-mails, a proposal, a letter of recommendation you wrote, and compare the styles. Probably you're subconsciously using different tones—*not* for different audiences, but for different genres. Pick the tone you like best and stick with it.

Exercise #2: Take one paragraph—especially one you don't like—and rewrite it in two or three different tones. Have some fun with it. Play around. See which option you like best. If you include the humorous tone in your experiment, you should have some interesting results.

In Closing...Web Thoughts

Websites are fast. Short. Exciting. They break the rules, play with words, do anything to create zip and jazz to keep the reader. Now for a reality check: people put hard copy on the Web, as is, and consider the job done. Then no one reads it and they waste a great opportunity to reach lots of people all at once. Should you have one hard copy and one Web copy of the same document? Maybe. Or better yet, relax the tone in both.

Section IV
Cohesive Structure:
Keeping It Together

Chapter 11
Seducing, Spinning, and Sedating:
All About Structure

Before we jump into the essentials of structure, let's confront the bad guys of word use: seducing and spinning. You've probably heard that wretched advertisers, unscrupulous lawyers, and con artists everywhere use them to deceive and otherwise rip you off. It's a corporate myth. If you want to write well, you *must* use these strategies. They're unavoidable, even when you're applying the near-angelic tenets of plain language.

Let's start with "seducing."

Seducing. I love the word, don't you? Seducing. It's so... seductive, so slippery, so sweet. Doubtless, one part seduction and one part word use and you think: subliminal seduction! That's how sneaky marketers embed suggestions into their message, so suddenly you're equating your basic pack of cigarettes with incredible sex. And your average burger and fries have orgasmic intensity. But only if you're lucky.

Alas, true "seducing" isn't nearly as provocative—especially in the cut-and-dried world of business writing. Whether you're writing a legalistic contract or a blurb for a cereal box top, your readers derive their own meaning from what you write. Typically, that meaning lies in what the words *don't* say, but what they suggest, implicate, or otherwise conjure.

Ernest Hemingway, borrowing from Freud, who borrowed from geographic fact, called this concept the "iceberg theory of writing." As everyone on the Titanic found out, an iceberg is a tiny little jut of ice with a mountain of mind-boggling proportions beneath it. Freud said the mind was like an iceberg: The conscious—what we know, see, observe, and think about—is the tip of the iceberg, but the real meaning is processed and held in that mountainous mass of our subconscious that lies far beneath.

Then Hemingway said words were the tip of the communications iceberg, but the real meaning—what they reader knew, felt, and assumed—was beneath the words; what the writer *didn't* say. Naturally, he was discussing literature, his in particular, which was famous for being sparse. Our mothers, in all their wisdom, put it more simply: "It isn't what you say; it's how you say it."

So to optimize your message, and the all-important response you get from the reader, you must seduce them with what you *don't* say and how you don't say it. For example, same meaning, different message:

> *No matter what some people think, Sunny Side Growers won't deliver produce to your house if you don't sign up by June 1. Just because we're a cooperative doesn't mean we make exceptions. We don't.*

The subliminal message: You're a jerk. Don't bug us. Nice, right? Of course, the subliminal message doesn't have to be that obvious. Here's another example:

> *According to Sunny Side Growers policy, we supply fresh produce to customers only if they sign an agreement form no later than June 1.*

Owing to the limitations of our delivery service, we are unable to accommodate requests after that point.

The subliminal message: A factory farm, mass-producing produce that might as well be in cans. We may grow vegetables for your family...but we're not your friend. Now look at this example:

Want us to deliver fresh vegetables to your door? Then sign up by June 1. We don't want to miss you!

This message is so pert and friendly, you'd practically expect Mr. Rogers to come knocking. Here is one more example:

What you say:

Please inform your employees about the new checks. We don't want them to mistake the bill for counterfeits and overwhelm us with calls and false alarms. It has a green background with pastel lettering and a tiny fruit fly design in the left corner.

What they think: Oh great. Another thing for me to worry about.

What you should say:

We wanted you to be the first to know the exciting news: We're introducing new checks with a green background, pastel lettering, and a colorful tiny fruit fly in the left corner. Pass the word to your employees too. We want them to appreciate the new checks and not confuse them with counterfeits.

Now, what they think: Wow, I'm the first to know! Can't wait to spread the good news.

Level of lying or misrepresenting the facts: 0.

Spinning. When people use the word "spinning" they don't actually mean "spinning." They're just using a euphemism for "lying," which sounds more professional and has a slightly scandalous edge. Lying, as everyone knows, is wrong. So think of spinning, the *real* spinning, as shifting information until the most important points land in the most important places. If the word "spinning" makes you feel queasy, replace it with "positioning."

How you position information determines how people to respond to it. Naturally, lots of "experts" have lots of expert opinions on the subject. For example, when I was a college professor, I attended innumerable workshops in which I learned the correct way to give students feedback. The strategy was pretty basic: Place good news first in the paragraph so the vulnerable student felt validated, open, and secure. Then, the student thus fortified, load on the bad! Sometimes that meant you wrote two positive lines and fifteen negatives. And usually, the student knew the strategy and skipped the positive to plunge into the icy cold misery of the negative anyway, but give us credit. We tried.

Here's how it looked:

> *Ted, I really like the way you describe your characters in this short story. David is so vivid, I can practically see him. But the plot needs to be more plausible—no one is seriously going to believe a well-respected medical student was dating an alien.*

Note another aspect of positioning: Downplay the negative, without sacrificing your point. You could have just as easily said:

> *Ted, plot in this story is totally implausible—no one will ever believe a well-respected medical student was dating an alien. No matter how good your descriptions, this aspect of the story is totally distracting.*

It wasn't just us college professors. Everyone, from preschool teachers through facilitators to marriage counselors, learned the same strategy. So you get comments such as:

> *Well, Beth and Don, I think it's just wonderful that you have lasted through 20 years of marriage. Your commitment to monogamy and family values is most impressive.*

Then, just as you're starting to feel good about your unhappy union, from the smiling lips of the marriage counselor comes the rest:

> *Only, to avoid enduring all the negativity and misery you have inflicted on each other during this time, you'll need couples counseling*

and individual therapy two to three days a week for the next five years.

Thanks, Doc.

Positioning can have an authentic value—one that can keep a reader from feeling undue misery, frustration, and panic. Remember the example I used earlier? About the senior citizen who received $450 too much in pension payments and would need to pay that amount back? Well, sometimes the amount was more—maybe $2,000 or $3,000. Typically, and sadly, my clients opened their letters with something like this:

According to our records, you received an overpayment of $4,000 which you must repay.

No "Hello, how are you?" No "Don't panic. I'm about to tell you something that sounds worse than it is." Just, "you received an overpayment of $4,000." Note, by the way, the word "overpayment." Not the friendliest or most assuring term. The financial equivalent of a Mack truck rolling over a tricycle.

You can imagine the shock and horror of the elderly persons who received this message. I don't know if this is rumor or what, but my clients claimed some recipients suffered heart attacks a few words in. If they didn't, the next line, the real blow, would have pushed them in that direction:

We will reclaim that amount immediately until the full amount is paid back.

Think the recipient stashed away those $4,000 for a sunny trip to Bermuda? Not so. That amount had accumulated over years in amounts so small no one noticed. And don't forget, many of these people had no other source of income. As for savings? No savings. And bills? Plenty of those. But wait—the story does have a happy ending—or would if they positioned their messages correctly.

My client had no intention of getting the $4,000 back all at once, but in small installments they deducted from the monthly checks. I don't remember the exact amount or how they calculated it. Let's say it was $20 a hit. So with careful positioning the letter could have read:

> *You will notice that your next pension check will be for $500 instead of $520. The reason is that you received too much money (what we call an "overpayment") in your checks for the last 10 years, amounting to $4,000. So we will deduct $20 a month until we get the $4,000 back.*

Granted, the news isn't great. But it's manageable. And if it isn't, the next line would also help—they can appeal the decision, contact their lawyer, and take other steps to ensure they get to keep that $20—which, by the way, many did.

Structure: The Great Unnatural Act

One cannot seduce with word use alone. That's where structure comes in. Place the most compelling, interesting, or funny information first, and up the likelihood the reader will form a positive impression. Make a promise up front, and they'll read to see how you'll keep it. Open with a boring preamble? Distressingly negative notes? Information that's all about you? About as seductive as a milk moustache. Then move the reader from point to point in such a logical yet delightful way, they'll never know they're reading.

Only one problem: structure doesn't come naturally. Think about your average conversation. You jump from one point to the next. Or even better, think about thinking. As in a meeting—you hear your boss say how the lab conditions are too cold and unpredictable to support a complete fruit fly community, and then you start thinking about...what you brought for lunch. Oh yes, you think, a peanut butter sandwich, then listen, what's this they're discussing? The budget, oh yes, that, then back to lunch and maybe you think about slipping out a get an Italian sub. With hot peppers. And mayo.

So how do you get control of this meandering mess? Keep reading. The answers lie ahead.

A Long Q&P Break

Listing—A Must-Do: When speaking, you say something and your listener nods. Say something else—they interrupt. When speaking to a group, they laugh, doze, and take notes or pass them. Either way, you know whether you've captivated your audience or lost them. Not so with writing. You must clinch your reader's attention—without ever knowing if you've clinched it. It's like shooting at a target, only you're in the dark and have no idea what the target looks like.

Your only hope—your best shot—is to create a smooth flow of tightly connected points that carries your readers from one scintillating and logical thought to the next. This structure, as I mentioned, is about as natural to you as sleep deprivation. So here's what you do. List the major points you want to cover in your message before you write. Don't outline. Don't plot. Just jot down a few quick words— we're talking short, clear, and easy to see.

Say you're drafting a report about Dr. Benson and the fruit fly catastrophe. Your list would look something like this:

◆ Study concept

◆ Conditions

◆ Impediments to conditions—lab technician

◆ Result

◆ Next steps

Finished with the list? Don't think you're finished. Because maybe this isn't the order you want. So reshuffle the list depending on a number of factors: the response you want, the concerns of the reader, or the most immediate point. So for example, I might reorder Dr. Benson's list this way:

- Result
- Impediments to conditions—lab technician
- Study concept
- Conditions
- Next steps

Remember: each bullet is not a sentence, paragraph, or even complete idea. They're the major points you want to mention—one could be three lines, the other could be two paragraphs. Then, write to the list. We'll look at lots of options for order in the next chapter; which one you choose is irrelevant as long as it works. If you have a longer document, draft two lists—one for the greater body and one for each section. If structure really *isn't* your forte, draft lists for long or complicated paragraphs too.

Here's how it looks:

Option 1:

In his study, Dr. Benson wanted to determine the reproductive habits of fruit flies to shed light on human beings' rituals concerning procreation. [study concept] *Naturally, the conditions differ—fruit flies, for example, don't meet in little bars or smoke tiny little cigarettes after consummation. However, both need a warm, preferably dry environment, although the drive is strong enough to resist even startlingly unfavorable conditions.* [conditions] *Unfortunately, one of the lab technicians left the air conditioner on all night in a full, frigid blast.* [impediments] *And frigid it was—not only did the fruit flies fail to procreate, but also a few dozen actually died.* [result] *Dr. Benson will have to import another batch of these specialty fruit flies, which will take over a month, and start the experiment from the beginning.* [next steps]

Option 2:

Last night, a few dozen of Dr. Benson's fruit flies died, and the rest remained in a chilly stupor, unable to interact with each other or even buzz around. [result] *The source of this misery was a lab technician who left the air conditioner on all night in a full, frigid blast.* [impediments] *This is bad news for Dr. Benson, who wanted to determine the reproductive habits of fruit flies to shed light on human beings' rituals concerning procreation.* [study concept] *Naturally, the conditions differ—fruit flies, for example, don't meet in little bars or smoke tiny little cigarettes after consummation. However, both need a warm, preferably dry environment, although their drive is strong enough to resist even startlingly unfavorable conditions.* [conditions] *Dr. Benson will have to import another batch of these specialty fruit flies, which will take over a month, and start the experiment from the beginning.* [next steps]

Listing: The Anti-ramble

So why list or plot? In a nutshell, you need to know where you're heading in order to get there, and those hazy cues in your brain won't help. Listing also has these distinct advantages:

1. Greater control. Once the copy is written—it's written. Rewriting for structure is too big, too difficult, and too hard for anyone to attempt.

2. Speed. No wasted time veering off to inconsequential points, and no repeated paragraphs or thoughts, which can add hours of writing time depending on the document.

3. Content. Everything's there—and where it ought to be—to drive your reader to that critical response because you determined order and content first.

Still not satisfied? Don't want to spend time listing? Read these Q&As to decide for sure:

Q&P Listing Q&As

Q. How much time will I need to write my list?

A. The list should take under a minute—although for longer documents expect a minute and a half. Need more time? Take it. It will save you on the writing end.

Q. How much detail should I include in my list?

A. Not much. A few words for each bullet is plenty.

Q. What if I *want* to include details?

A. Go ahead. Just don't add so many details that you clutter the list.

Q. What if my list isn't in the order I want?

A. That's exactly the point. Just reorder them on your list. You can either cut and paste them if you're on the computer, or renumber your items if you're using paper.

Q. Should I collect information before or after I write my list?

A. Good question. Do whatever works for you; either way, you can always adjust the list as content or desire dictates.

Reading Reality Check

Having said all that about structure, let's taste a slice of reading reality. Here's what happens:

Opening paragraph: The reader reads more of this paragraph than any other—and with greater attention. No surprise: this is the most critical part of your document.

Middle paragraphs: Let's be real. Few people read the whole thing. In fact, hardly anyone reads long documents from cover to cover, and few people read a one-pager from top to bottom. With the Web, you have a better chance of sustaining the visitor's interest from point to point, but that's because they're getting bite-size and highly digestible morsels as they click from page to page. Naturally, this leads to two questions:

Q. If my readers don't pay attention to the middle section, then I guess I can write in whatever style I want, right?

A. Wrong. Your readers don't read, but your readers do skim. Which means they'll dip in to your writing, read the points that most interest them, then resurface, and dip in again. The better the writing, the more they'll dip.

Q. But does structure really matter? I mean, if they're flitting...

A. Yes, structure matters—it matters even more— because the reader needs to know where they're heading without having to read. A good, clean structure helps them predict.

Q. Excellent point. How about endings—does anyone even look at those?

A. I'll get to that in a moment.

Endings: Rumor has it some readers concentrate on the beginning and end of a document and dabble in the middle. My experience says forget the ending. Once readers get what they need, they quit. But just in case your readers doggedly read through every word, keep the endings tight and succinct.

Repeat Structure Repeats

You may be wondering whether you need to repeat points if your reader jumps around, glancing at some sections and skipping the rest. And what about those Websites where the readers sample the message but don't dwell? Will they miss major points? Or do you risk boring them with repeats?

Good question. Here's the answer: That depends —on the message, the reader, and how important or detailed the information is. If you must, restate core ideas, identify important concepts, and explain sticky terms, but stop there. And keep it fast!

Closing Big Picture Question:
A Personal Question to the Author

Q. You said people don't read from beginning to end. Think anyone will read this book from beginning to end?

A. Hmm...good question. Hopefully, some people will find the writing so witty, provocative, and important that they'll savor every word and read from the first word of the introduction to the last in Chapter 13. But I'm a realist, and know plenty of readers will jump around to the parts that interest them most. Either way, I'd love to hear about *your* writing habits, which leads us to...

The Next Q&P Tell-All

What are your reading habits? Are you a linear reader? Do you jump around? Do you prefer the Web? Hard copy? How did you reach *this* part of the book? If you read the whole thing, then you know where to go to send an answer: *www.quickandpainlessbusinesswriting.com.*

Chapter 12
The Paragraph:
On Closer Inspection

Paragraph Myth and Reality: A Jet Back in Time

Okay, back, back, back to high school again. Yup, there she is: Miss Ferguson, teaching...what's this? Paragraph structure? And she's telling you to read the paragraph on—how ironic!—paragraph structure. Probably it sounded like something from Prentice-Hall's high school textbook. It has an alluring and charming name that must have set the young students on fire: *Grammar and Composition*. Could they make it any more boring? Unless, of course, you consider the writing in the actual book. Here's what it says:

A paragraph usually has one sentence that states the main idea of the paragraph. The other sentences explain, support, and develop the main idea with examples, details, facts, reasons, or an incident.

The text, in its usual scintillating style, continues to discuss the topic sentence, the support sentences, and the concluding sentences, which tells young readers:

A concluding sentence completes a paragraph by summarizing the ideas and sometimes restating the topic sentence in different words.

Which is, as you know by now, exactly what you *shouldn't* do.

Now flash forward: The present. Pick up your local newspaper. Pick up *Time* magazine. Pick up anything. See any topic sentences? Any concluding sentences? Nope, because they're not there. They don't exist in the real world. A paragraph may bundle thoughts together, but whether you open with a topic sentence, continue a thought, or just give support, that's up to you.

The Paragraph–Brick Connection

Paragraphs are the bricks holding your document together and the transitions are the mortar. If that metaphor wasn't enough, let's extend it further. Because, as you'll see, you have countless choices about how to structure your paragraphs as long as your points connect. Your points don't hold together? No problem. Draft lists for each one.

Okay, this prospect might make you feel tired, disheartened, and overwhelmed. So let's compromise. Only list certain paragraphs—long or complex ones, for example, or paragraphs where the information just isn't coming together for mysterious reasons. And only list until your structure problem goes away for good and the order flows naturally.

Let's look at some basics about paragraph structure:

Keep it clean. No one likes a rag-tag message, pieces flying all over the place. It's chaotic, disorderly, and distasteful. It's the equivalent of a seducer with bad breath, body odor, and fuzzy teeth. No, the flow of information must be smooth, moving from point to point as effortlessly as a waltz. The trick is in two parts:

Part 1: Make sure your points are in a logical order within the entire document as well as within the paragraph. Move chronologically, carrying your points effortlessly through time, or compare points one by one. Doesn't matter. Just make sure they make sense.

Part 2: Use "transitions." These are the glue words holding the paragraph together. With chronological order, you use time, as in: 3:00, 4:00, and 5:00, or winter, spring, and fall. When comparing, you use transitions such as "in contrast" or "on the other hand."

The variety–spice equation. Think variety. Eight-line-long paragraphs, then bullets, then short paragraphs, then Q&As. Seduce them with the scenery. They'll love it.

Keep it short. Yes, variety. But not long variety. Short variety. Cut your paragraphs at eight lines—opt for five when possible. Have a 20-line paragraph? Break it in three. But don't be skimpy— that's cheesy. Have a one-line paragraph? Tack it onto the one before or after it. As for the message itself—here are some length pointers:

Letters. Stick with the slim 'n' trim one-pagers, using five paragraphs tops. Here's what it contains:

The Introduction
   Length: Five lines max.
   Contains: Most important point in the usual awe-inspiring way

The Body
   Length: Three paragraphs max, no more than eight (okay 10, if you must) lines each. That's *lines*, not sentences.
   Contains: Support or additional information

The Closing
   Length: Two to three lines
   Contains: Follow-up information, such as how your readers can reach you, when, or what you plan to do next.

Oh, and limit the letter to one page. It's psychological. Readers see two pages and consider your message needy, high maintenance, too much to read. But say you have two or three pages of information to cover? What then? Write the choice bits on the letter and add the rest in enclosures.

Web. With the Web, your reader has ADHD *and* amnesia. So keep it fast. Use bite-size pieces of, say, five or six lines with reminders, snappy headers, lots of bullets and plenty of breaks.

And remember: it's harder to read on the computer screen than on paper, so make sure short=shorter with plenty of eye-friendly white space.

E-mails. Two or three paragraphs, tops. As for the rest, think attachment.

Reports, proposals, and other SERIOUS messages. Short paragraphs, plenty of punchy sub-heads, lots of white space, and visual enhancement like graphs, charts, and even sidebars.

Marketing materials. Have fun—wild opening, zesty quotes, Q&As—the possibilities are endless. But keep it short; each paragraph should average four lines, five max.

In the Beginning...The Pre-paragraph

You must have skipped most of this book if you don't realize your openings matter most. More than your charts, graphs, just about anything. If you have a Website, you may think your opening—or that first impression—lies in the home page, but you're wrong. Ask yourself this: If you want to find a dentist, whose Website would you explore? The dentist at *www.pullnpoke.com* or *www.professionaldentistry.com*?

Hre are some pointers about openings of all types:

Web Words Protocol

Your Web address should have these qualities:

◆ **Say-ability:** Opt for a name that anyone can say—which means numbers, weird combinations, and other twists are definitely out.

◆ **Memorable:** If they can't say it, they won't remember it. See above.

◆ **Distinct:** If you're using your own name, then distinct may not work in your favor, particularly if it's Bill Kennedy, Bob Jones, or Mohammad just about anything. (Mohammad is supposedly the most popular man's name in the world.) But if you have a choice, opt for something with zing.

◆ **Informative:** Provide information when possible. Cut hair? How about *www.beautifulcuts.com*? The idea works even better if your salon has the same name. Located somewhere fashionable? Cool, then try something such as: *www.beautifulcutsnyc.com*. All the information they need to know is there.

◆ **Keep it short.** Short=say-able, memorable, distinct. Tempting though it may be, ignore any impulses that lead you to combinations like this one: *www.beautifulcutsnewyorkcity&syracuse.com*.

Subject Lines: Quick, Clean, and Clever

Creating successful subject lines can make learning ancient Greek seem easy. You have just three or four words—one wrong choice and the subject line wilts. Here are the five most pertinent pointers:

1. **Reader-focus**—always, everything, reader-focused. Vive la difference:

   Do: *Exciting seminar! Don't miss out!*
   Not: *Department-sponsored training*

2. **Provide information.**

   Do: *Your fruit fly expertise wanted*
   Not: *Meeting please attend*

3. **Use fast, fizzy words**—don't worry about grammar.

   Do: *Penalties ahead—watch out*
   Not: *Penalty policy implementation*

4. **Mention repercussions...nicely.** The first example about reader-focus did precisely that. Here's another example:

   Do: *Don't miss fruit fly farm*
   Not: *Department outing*

5. **Humor's okay,** depending on your reader.

   Do: *Fruit fly pops, anyone?*
   Not: *Death of fruit flies*

Summaries? Overviews? Introductions?

Write reports, letters, press releases, or virtually any other prescribed documents? Then someone else—or the unknown forces that dictate workplace writing—may dictate where you place information and how. But assuming the document is yours, here's how you manage the three most overlooked, underdone, and frequently unnecessary paragraphs: summaries, overviews, and introductions.

Summaries

This tight, information-packed paragraph belongs at the beginning of your document—although some opt for the end. Use it when

1. you have so many points the reader can't keep track;
2. your document is so long, long, long the reader will never get through the major points;
3. your reader wants a crash course rather than read the whole document;
4. your reader needs a guide to determine what to read and what to ignore.

List key points only, drop details, keep it short—a paragraph or two is plenty. And avoid these summary mistakes:

Mistake: Focus on one or two points and forget the rest.

Mistake: Discuss points in a different order from what's in the text.

Mistake: Use half-sentences, fragments, rambling long sentences and other creative devices owing to poor writing and questionable strategy.

So when do you put summaries at the end? That depends; usually form dictates. Academic pieces usually have the little wrap-up at the end, primarily because the author has made more important points than the reader can remember and needs a refresher before going forward. Others summarize to clarify a set of complex points. But whether you're using a summary to open or close, remember: Less is better.

Here's a sample about a company called Delta Oil and Gas, known mostly for its tarnished reputation. The author is a consultant brought in to determine why that reputation is so bad:

Three factors figure into Delta's negative reputation. One is Delta's pricing, which, as reports indicate, has been excessive. Second is Delta's previous spate of advertising—"If you don't like the prices at the pump, then walk," and the follow-up "Heating Costs Too High? Wear a Sweater." And third, CEO Ron Butterly's publicized affair with Diamond Production's CEO Terry McDaniel, which some suggest led to the two companies merging. You can address and subdue these issues with a renewed PR and advertising campaign that focuses on the company's philanthropic efforts.

Overviews

These panoramic landscapes have high boring-potential, although they can be a good setting-setter, with these qualities:

- ◆ **Specificity.** Watch for general language and general points that sedate the reader in all the wrong ways. Keep it clean, vivid, and real.

- ◆ **Context.** So what exactly is Delta's problem? And even more importantly, what is the solution that would propel them into a better, brighter future? Context tells all.

- ◆ **Newness.** Say something new to the reader— always. Or if you ache to show the reader you understand them, their business, and so on, say something *new* about something old.

Here's a sample:

To address the current spate of negative publicity Delta Oil and Gas has recently suffered, we conducted focus groups and examined hundreds of articles about the subject. As we will discuss, several issues are at the heart of these problems: Delta's pricing; Delta's previous advertising campaigns; and CEO Ron Butterly's publicized affair with Diamond Production's CEO Terry McDaniel, which some suggest led to the two companies merging. We will examine these issues in detail and provide recommendations about how you can overcome these barriers to become the nation's preeminent oil and gas provider, making Exxon and Amoco as relevant to our nation's fuel requirements as firewood.

First (Introductory) Paragraphs

Your first paragraph introduces the subject at hand. You have no choice—it's the first thing the reader sees. Every first paragraph needs a "gun" and every gun needs a first paragraph to holster it. So what's a gun? Good question.

Think about mysteries. You open the book: Chapter I. Our hero enters the room. Strips off her clothes, rolls them in a ball, and shoves them in a corner. Takes the gun from her purse and puts it in a drawer. Then naked, beat-up, exhausted, but satisfied that the last case is finally over, falls into deep sleep. What happens next is practically irrelevant. You know that gun is in the drawer, and at some point, our hero will use it. Maybe twice. Whatever the reason, it's worth waiting for.

Sadly (or not) most of your content won't involve weapons, nudity, or dirty clothes. But you should still place a figurative gun in the opening—the reader will read and read, or at least skim and skim, until it goes off. What are these guns? Lots of things, such as:

Numbers. You could start a document with a straight statement of fact, as in this gun-less version:

> *Because issues surrounding Delta are so sensitive, Ron Butterly should keep a low profile. Delta should also refrain from any advertising for at least a month, before embarking on its 'We're philanthropic' campaign.*

Boring? Well, yes, but even worse, it misses an enormous opportunity to build a little tension. Here's what the author could have said:

> *Because issues surrounding Delta are so sensitive, the company must take four critical steps or their problems will only deepen. First, Ron Butterly should keep a low profile. Second, Delta should also refrain from any advertising for at least a month, before embarking on its 'We're philanthropic' campaign...*

Promises. Basically, we're talking about business-writing bribery. Don't feel bad—plenty of perfectly good people have used this device to astonishing ends. Even better, your readers will have no idea you're using it. Basically, the strategy comes down to this:

If they read your copy, they'll get something good at the end. Here goes:

> *Delta has a serious problem. A problem that threatens the organization's future. But there are solutions—solutions that could launch Delta's image beyond its heyday in 1949. How do you get there? The road map to success will be revealed in the following pages.*

Questions. With questions, the reader wants an answer and will read to get it. Just make sure the question's good. None of the obvious stuff of the "Do you want to save money?" variety. Who'd ever say no? Besides, you should avoid questions for which the answer can be yes or no. Instead use provocative questions, including:

> *How long will it take Delta to revive? Three years? Five? More? The answer may surprise you—but not half as much as the strategies involved in getting you there. And many of them begin in Tennessee.*

Opening Paragraph Possibilities—In Closing

Here are some other possibilities for a snazzy opening:

Descriptive Openings

Tarlotte, Tennessee, is a small, unassuming town. It has a town hall, two churches, a library, and a dozen or so stores along the main street. To the east is the Tarlotte River—to the west, a low range of mountains. And sandwiched in between, on the outskirts of Tarlotte, is an unexpected sight: a Delta oil refinery. This is only one reason why Tarlotte went from being a nameless town to an example of how Delta can find natural resources in unexpected places.

Metaphors

Tarlotte, Tennessee, is a jigsaw puzzle. The pieces seem separate and scattered, but put them together and this little town can resolve some of the most perplexing enigmas facing the oil industry today.

Quotes
> *John Kennedy said: "Ask not what your country can do for you, but what you can do for your country." And the people of Tarlotte, Tennessee, have applied his words to an altogether new kind of national threat: low fuel resources.*

Questions
> *What is Tarlotte, Tennessee? A humble town? Or a prototype for the future of oil and gas? The answers are as vital as they are perplexing.*

Beyond the Beginning: Imposing Order

Most- to Least-important

Of all the orders you can pick for your paragraph, one reigns supreme: presenting the most important information first, aka most- to least-important order. What's most important depends on your audience and what they most need to know. Sounds like reader-focus, right? That's right. Look at the difference in these paragraphs:

> **To: Employees entering Delta's home office**
> *The security procedures have changed after the recent spate of negative PR on May 15. Now you must show your identification at the security desk just beyond the gate. Be sure to carry your driver's license or one other form of identification, as you may need to present that too. Your visitors should present their identification before entering the gate and should wait in the outer lobby area for an escort. You must take these procedures seriously—any violations are punishable by law.*
> **Most important point:** *Employees and visitors must show ID to enter the building every day.*

> **To: Visitors**
> *When arriving at the gate, present your identification to the guard who will allow you in—then wait for your escort in the outer lobby. Escorts must be employees who have valid identification, which they*

will need to show to sign you in. You must take these procedures seriously—any violations are punishable by law.
Most important point: *Visitors need to check in and have an escort. The memo doesn't say the requirements are new, as visitors don't know the old ones.*

To: Security
The security procedures have changed as of May 15 owing to the spate of negative PR. Contact the military police immediately if visitors or employees fail to comply. All employees must now show identification at the security desk just beyond the gate and a driver's license or another form of identification, if their identification is close to the expiration date or otherwise causes suspicion. Check the identification of all visitors before the gate and send them to the outer lobby to wait for an escort.
Most important point: *There are new security measures, so be alert—and nab 'em if you need to.*

The Inverted Pyramid

Journalists call the most- to least-important information order the "inverted pyramid," and they use it with every hard news story—those events fresh off the press. So what do they put in the first paragraph? What journalists call the Five Ws: the Who, What, When, Where, Why, and How of the story. Okay, you may be wondering why you have *six* "Ws" and one begins with an "H." Good question. Don't ask.

Analysis and Support

If you make a point, you need to support it. You do this naturally—especially when you're enraged. Think about your average lovers' quarrel. It goes something like this:

She: *You're a slob, and I'm sick of picking up after you.* [point] *You leave your underwear on the floor of the bathroom every morning after you take a shower,* [support] *and you don't rinse the hairs out of the sink after you shave. So I get treated to looking at little hairs every time I brush my teeth.* [support]

195

He: *I'm a slob? Look who's talking?* [point] *You leave your hairbrush loaded with hair on the bathroom shelf* [support] *and little piles of clothes scattered about the bedroom because you can't decide what to wear when you wake up.* [support]

Naturally, the beauty of lovers' quarrels is their ludicrous nature. She could just ask him to pick up his underwear. As for him—the fact that *she* might be a slob doesn't make him less of one. So the argument's pretty thin. Here's another example.

The Chocolate Company of Nebraska has created what they call a unique "health bar." [point] *Like other chocolate bars this one tastes delicious. And it contains antioxidants.* [support] *But the unique aspect of their candy creations lies in the nut and nugget mix. These hard chunks embedded in soft chocolate scrape away plaque and other hazardous substance from the teeth.* [support] *Even better, the nuts are a marvelous source of protein.* [support]

The structure of this paragraph would look like this:
Point
Support
Support

Q&P Paragraph Reminder: Look!

In the real world of writing, size counts. Only this time, the bigger, the worse: Your paragraphs should be in small chunks, not mammoth blocks of text. So how do you cram a point *plus* support into a single paragraph? If you have two bits of support as in the chocolate company example, don't worry about it. But three, four, or five items? End the paragraph at support point two and start a new paragraph or two for points three, four, and five. Your structure would look like this:

Paragraph I
Point
Support
Support

Paragraph II
Support
Support
Support

In the chocolate company example, paragraph two would look like this:

Another, lesser known aspect of the Chocolate Company of Nebraska's health food success: they add Vitamin C and D to every chocolatey batch. [support] *In fact, one of their Nicer Nuts bars has more Vitamin D than a full glass of milk.* [support] *And let's not forget the added benefits of their special Cherry Nutter bars that have highly nutritious ground-up freeze-dried cherry bits.* [support]

Of course, you don't *have* to start with your point. In fact, sometimes it's better to offer support and *then* make your point. In that case, your structure will look like this:

Paragraph
Support
Support
Support
Point

Use this structure when the support is more convincing and compelling than the point. Here's an example:

Fatigue can take a toll—it can destroy your work Quick and Painless Business WritingFive No-Worry Reality Checks life. [support] *Wear down your relationship with your spouse and kids.* [support] *And it can take a toll your health—causing you to get colds, headaches, and countless other ailments.* [support] *That's why keeping your energy level high with a daily snack of the Chocolate Company's select brand of health bars is so important.* [point]

Paragraph Length: How to Tell...

Do what my editor did when I was a journalist ages go. Back then only the spies on *Get Smart* used computers, and cable was something that was buried underground. He took my paragraphs, counted the lines to five and started a new paragraph. Maybe he looked for a transition that would make a clean break; maybe not. It was just one, two, three...break. That's what he did. And those were the days when things were *slow*!

Final Word on the Final Word: Why Paragraph Length Matters

So why does size count? Remember those textbooks in high school and college? Loaded with long paragraphs that basically formed a sheet of ink on the page? How'd you feel when you saw them waiting? Overjoyed? Enthusiastic? Did you rush to read every black-inked word? Obviously not. And neither will your reader.

Today's Mantra

White space, white space, white space.

The Big Four: Equal Facts, Chronological, Descriptive, Compare and Contrast

Now for more paragraph possibilities—and what could be better than the old standard: equal facts?

1. Equal Facts: Your Own Best Friend

You use the equal-facts order all the time, when all your points are equal. Take your shopping list for the supermarket. Need eggs more than milk? Chicken more than bread? Who knows? Equal facts. In business writing, the equal facts might read this way:

As Blair probably told you, we have a great idea for developing a fabulous new kids' toy we're calling a Spooze Ball. It's different from your ordinary softball because it has a doughy texture. This makes the ball hilariously unpredictable and can lead to great marketing schemes. As for the color—no boring whites or grays. These are lime green and sunshine yellow.

You can write your equal facts list many ways. For example, you could make an actual list that goes down the page:

We have a great idea—a Spooze Ball. It's different from your ordinary softball because:

1. *Its texture is heavier—almost doughy;*

2. *It's unpredictable—great marketing possibilities; and*

3. *The colors aren't boring whites or grays but way-out and wacky lime green and sunshine yellow.*

If you're in a hurry, save yourself the trouble of numbers, transitions, and full sentences, and throw in some semicolons:

We have a great idea for developing a fabulous new kids' toy we're calling a Spooze Ball. It has a heavier, almost doughy texture; is hilariously unpredictable, which can lead to great marketing possibilities; and the colors are a way-out and wacky lime green and sunshine yellow.

As for the response—it would go something like this:

Kids will mistake it for Play-Doh, or worse, cookie dough, and try to eat it. I can just see the lawsuits. No go on the Spooze Ball. Try again.

Equal Facts: The Bullets

Another flashback—although it may not be your flashback if you're young. In the days of typewriters and Wite-Out, no one used bullets. That's because no one *had* bullets. Instead, we used numbers and dashes, but mostly paragraphs. Once computers came in, bulleting spread like a germ. But germs, such as cholesterol, come in good and bad forms—or at least in our book they do. Here's why:

The good germ: Bullets let you separate out information into tidy, digestible nuggets—a requirement for today's ADHD reader. The paragraphs look slim and approachable, and the main points, normally squelched among countless insignificant words, will stand out. Besides, with bullets you don't have to write in full sentences!

The bad germ: Everyone uses them. Your average brochure—a collection of bulleted lists. A report? Bulleted lists. Everything bulleted lists. Worse, people didn't know how to use them, so you had loads of bulleted lists that didn't make sense.

The *really* bad germ: During the Clinton/Gore administration's attempts to create better, more understandable text using plain language, some in the federal government got a great idea: If bullets are good once, they *must* be good *all* the time. So they stuck them in every document, at the beginning of *every* paragraph. In regulations, grant applications, notices—you name it. There they were, great big rambling paragraphs and dots next to them. Perplexed, some readers assumed the feds had format and design problems.

Bullets: The Use and Misuse

So when do you use bullets: with three or more points that might get lost in a paragraph? The operative word here is *power*. Use verbs to launch every new bullet and steer clear of boring openings and repeated words. Look:

YES: *Over the next few months, I will:*

- *Draft the Spooze Ball marketing plan,*
- *Create a working Spooze Ball tagline and logo, and*
- *Find a Spooze Ball jingle no kid can resist.*

NO: *Over the next few months:*

- *I will draft the Spooze Ball marketing plan,*
- *I will create a working Spooze Ball tagline and logo, and*
- *I will find a Spooze Ball jingle no kid can resist.*

And look—each verb is in the same tense. Here's an example of **what not to do:**

NO: *Over the next few months, I will:*

◆ *Be drafting the Spooze Ball marketing plan,*

◆ *Create a working Spooze Ball tag line and logo, and*

◆ *I need to talk to the guys in Music so they can develop a Spooze Ball jingle no kid can resist.*

2. Chronological and Sequential Order

Next to the equal-facts order, chronological order is easiest to create. That's because you approach it the way you do life: chronologically. You wake up at 6:00, have breakfast by 6:30, and leave for work at 7:00. At work, in e-mails and reports, you probably already use chronological order. Your transitions would include months, weeks, days, and even hours. Here's one example:

When we first entered Lotterdame City, nothing seemed unusual. Within three days, however, we noticed unrest. The locals seemed to avoid us and would vanish for no known reason. Within a month, we started identifying trends. Over the next four months, we monitored this situation closely and have recorded our findings in this report.

Typically, you will use chronology when giving directions, possibly in an easy-to-read list such as this one:

When feeding fish:
Step 1: Get out the fish food.
Step 2: Wave your hand and sing a little so the fish know you're there.
Step 3: Scatter the food in the water.

By the way, you can never be too careful with instructions—the reader knows less than you think.

Naturally, some e-mails contain chronology like this one: I plan to present the report about Lotterdame City at 1:15 so I can join Scotty and the Secret Association of International Spies by 4:00. If people need me then, I will be indisposed please shoot them if they press for information. Between 6:00 and 7:00, I'll have dinner at the usual place underground, then will work at an undisclosed location. I'll leave that undisclosed location to sleep at another undisclosed location at 11:00.

Notice: the time transitions appear at different parts of the sentence. For example, the transition "1:15" rests in the middle and "4:00" at the end of the sentence. Yet, "6:00" sprouts up at the beginning of the sentence, and that final "11:00" at the end. Feel free to move your transitions to different parts of the sentence—it adds variety. You could be more general in your transitions, too. For example, you may say: "I usually stay at home in the morning and arrive at work in mid-afternoon."

3. Descriptive

This is the sleeper structure—it has loads of possibilities and can apply to abstractions (such as proposals), or concrete items. And you can describe them in innumerable different ways. Here's just a sample:

Large-to-Small

Give the most sweeping point first, then narrow down to particulars that either support the general point or add new information. You can use this order with just about anything, from a responsibility to a physical object. Here's one example:

When searching a room, scope out the full dimensions. How high is the ceiling? How thick are those walls? Then check the floorboards for cracks. See any loose panels in the desk or drawers? How about the telephones? The computer keyboard? What's beneath every A-B-C could spell trouble.

Most- to Least- or Least- to Most-Noticeable

This descriptive device may seem like general-to-specific—but it's far more intriguing. Let's start with a physical object such as a vase I recently bought. Here's what I might say, from most- to least-noticeable:

The vase is Romanesque with a large, cup-like top, and two gold handles. At the bottom is a thin stem and a black square base. If you look closely, you'll see a tiny line between the stem and the base— no thicker than a hair. This could be home to illegal substances, microchips, and other items an agent should detect.

Here's one more example—this time in a least- to most-noticeable order:

She's malicious—so you'd better be careful. The moment you leave the room, she'll insult you. And secrets? She'll tell your secrets to everyone, exaggerating the problems and throwing in subtle insults. Yet she's so well dressed, well mannered, and socially correct, you immediately trust her.

4. Compare and Contrast

You definitely remember the compare and contrast structure from high school. Who doesn't? It was so versatile—coming in handy in the debate club (the Democrats' versus the Republicans' stance on just about anything), science projects (before you put the dye on the frog's corpse and after), and literature (comparing Kurt Vonnegut to Emily Dickinson). Invite this structure into these documents:

- ◆ Proposals—how things are now and how much better they'll be once you're through with them.

- ◆ Reports—how things *were* first, then later.

- ◆ E-mails—how things *might* be if the reader doesn't hurry up and respond versus how things *should* be.

- ◆ Letters—all of the above.

The compare/contrast notion goes by many other names, all tempting the reader to read on. You have the functional "Problem and Solution" order and the intrigue of "Myth and Reality." Then, there's the ever-convincing "Before and After" example advertisers for diet products like so much. Or try your basic "Then and Now" approach. Either way, you can draft your comparisons in many ways. Here's a sample:

Structure 1: Compare points line by line.

When to use: When you have longer points or images that you want to compare.

Roadmap: If you drew a roadmap of this structure, your order would look like this:

a–b, a–b, a–b…

See if you can identify the a–b structure here:

When thinking about a career as an international spy, consider all factors. The work is exciting and fast-paced, but you won't get to tell anyone about it—not even your mother or your spouse. You'll travel to exotic lands, see incredible scenery, meet interesting people, and sample unusual foods. Only some, if not all, of the local population will try to kill you. Finally, you will be working for your nation, protecting everyone in the free land. Only you won't get any honors or awards for your efforts—you won't even get to write a book about it later.

Structure 2: Compare one set of points all at once; then another.

When to use: When you have short points that you want to compare.

Roadmap: Clump the points together, weighing one side of the argument against the other.

Roughly, it looks like:

a–a–a, b–b–b…

Notice the difference:

When thinking about a career as an international spy, consider all factors. The work is exciting and fast-paced. You'll travel to exotic lands, see incredible scenery, meet interesting people, and sample unusual foods. And, perhaps most importantly, you will be working for your nation, protecting everyone in the free land. On the negative side, you won't get to tell anyone about your job—not your mother or your spouse. Wherever you go, some, if not all, of the local population will hope to kill you. As for awards and honors? No awards, no honors. You won't even get to write a book about it later.

Structure 3: Cluster one set of points in one or two paragraphs and the other set of points in the following one or two paragraphs

When to use: When you have one point that requires a great deal of support.

Roadmap: This one's really spread out. So much for the topic sentence idea. Here's what you get, more or less:

a–a–a–a–a
a–a–a–a–a
a–a–a–a–a
b–b–b–b–b
b–b–b–b–b
b–b–b–b–b

This arrangement works best when you provide lots of details to support your point. Here's an example—a personal favorite. I'm comparing writing to editing:

> *With writing, determine what response you want from your message first. Then, write the document. Don't worry about making every word perfect—just get the thoughts down now. Most people like to leave their message a while before revising. Be sure to revise for mistakes you've made in the past and don't try to correct for everything all at once.*

> *Editing is different. The message is already written; your job is to make it better. Your best strategy is to read a few paragraphs and get a sense of the author's strengths and weaknesses. Then, correct the mistakes. Once you're done, double-check your changes. Also, let the author know his or her weaknesses. This will help him or her become a better writer.*

And Now For a Reality Slice: The Un-paragraph

Yes, your garden-variety paragraphs with the topic, support, and concluding sentences are a little archaic. So are paragraphs composed of one structure, such as a straight compare-and-contrast or that descriptive paragraph we talked about earlier. Most paragraphs nowadays combine structures, blending compare-and-contrast with descriptive and countless other possibilities. You could call them un-paragraphs. Just make sure the points follow a sound, logical order, no matter where they go.

Mix 'n' Match Paragraphs: The Examples

Say you're an investigator and the guy you're going to tail is Larry (not his real name). You could open with this multi-approach description:

Larry is a family man with two children and a home in Smallville. No question, the guy's a professional. He worked for nine of the top 10 companies in his field and knows more about your computer system than your IT experts. Wherever his dough comes from, he gets plenty of it: He lives in a mansion with an endless driveway, Buckingham Palace–style gardens, and a wraparound porch about a mile long. But trust him? Hey, the guy's a menace.

Can you see the structures at work here? You open with your support—a list of Larry's attributes in equal-facts order:

◆ a family man

◆ a professional

◆ rich

Then, the structure switches to a descriptive order from the front of his property to the inside of his house:

◆ long driveway

◆ fancy gardens

◆ wrap-around porch

Then, you end with your main point: the guy's a menace. The remaining paragraphs tell why. So your structure might look like this:

Support 1—equal facts
Support 2—equal facts
Support 3—equal facts
Support 4—descriptive
Support 5—descriptive
Support 6—descriptive
Support 7—descriptive
Point

Q&P Break

Look at the paragraphs in this book for style. Or open a magazine or newspaper. Notice the devices, the variety, the way they pull in transitions to glue the whole thing together. By noticing, you'll start to pick up these good habits. As for this paragraph? Chronological order with a Q&A twist at the end.

Q&P Transition Tips

Let's get back to the brick and mortar metaphor. Bricks are the sentences in the paragraph—transitions the mortar holding them together. They can be glue words, like conjunctions and prepositions, or full-fledged phrases. Here are some tips:

Tip #1: Think discreet.

These critical (albeit boring) words bring as much spark to a message as dust. So don't be obvious. Slip them in discreetly and opt for short one- or two-word transitions. Look:

Do: "Advertisers get you to show up for sales by pretending their sales are exclusive. How many times have you seen those very words: 'Exclusive Sale: Today Only,' for example? Or how about those so-called membership deals? Sign up to be a 'member' of their club and you get to shop in their store. Of course, you know the membership is phony. Who has ever been *rejected* from their club?"

Not: "Advertisers get you to show up for sales by pretending their sales are exclusive. One example that comes to mind is the signs that say those very words: 'Exvusive Sale: Today Only.' Another example that probably seems familiar is those membership deals—you sign up to be a 'member' of their club and you get to shop in their store. Of course, as you probably know, the membership is phony. Ask yourself this question: Who has ever been *rejected* from their club?"

Tip #2: Variety counts.

Vary everything! In Tip #1, the transitions morphed from sentences to questions. This gives your message a nice rhythm and more interesting word-use possibilities. If you're writing a piece in equal-facts order, scatter the numerical transitions, leaving some at the beginning and others at the end of the sentence. Sometimes you can even get away with being inconsistent. Here's an example:

Do: "The first thing I noticed was the mossy covering on the pile of dirt. Looking closer, I saw little black dots. What were these? Mold? Strange plants of some sort? I got a shovel and dug a little. Yep, Johnston had been growing rare, medicinal mushrooms before he died, and in a few weeks they'd be ready to harvest."

Not: "The first thing I noticed was the mossy covering on the pile of dirt. The second thing I noticed, looking closer, was little black dots. Third,

I wondered, 'What were these? Mold? Strange plants of some sort?' Fourth, I got a shovel and dug a little. Finally, I concluded that Johnston had been growing the rare, medicinal mushrooms before he died, and in a few weeks they'd be ready to harvest."

Tip #3: Use the transition litmus test.

Consider this a Q&P break, too. Look at something you wrote recently. Look at an individual paragraph or an entire page. See transitions? If the answer is yes—chances are your structure is strong. If not, you have a problem. Go back and list.

Chapter 13
The End

Here we are—at the shortest chapter of this book, our last lesson, and our goodbye. No surprise; we've been writing about endings. These verbal plugs aren't exactly magical; in fact, in most cases they're unnecessary. If you're writing and there's nothing else to say, just stop.

Let's look at this book for a case study. I started by giving a big picture of writing issues you should remember as we moved along. Then, I went from smaller issues (word use), to bigger issues (tone), to more pervasive and sweeping issues (structure). Now I'm at the last part of a well-structured piece: endings. What more to say? I said all I intended. I have the right number of words my publisher requested for the book. So what's next? A wrap-up.

If your form or circumstance does require a closing, here are some pointers:

Summaries

We talked about these before—especially when they open a document. You can end with a summary on three occasions:

1. When your boss requires you to do so.

2. When you have a five-page or longer piece jam-packed with information and know the reader won't read from beginning to end.

3. When you have connecting points too complex or numerous for the reader to absorb. In white papers (such as government reports or any authoritative document, for those lucky laypeople unfamiliar with the term) or research papers, you can write summaries after every section.

No matter why you're writing, keep summaries

◆ fast—focus on key points but not support;

◆ short—no longer than a paragraph;

◆ chronological—review your points in the order you made them.

Conclusions

Conclusions are strange. They take lots and lots of points and draw a conclusion based on each of them. In high school, we marked their presence with the transition "in conclusion..." So when should you conclude? Aside from when your boss makes you? Here's when:

◆ You have a short document with lots of interesting points that the reader can't help but read...leading to an even more interesting conclusion.

- You have a really great, really persuasive introduction, with a compelling gun. You might say
  something like: "Our research unearthed some
  truly mind-boggling findings." Your reader may
  read through each of the interesting points to
  reach that climactic end.

- You have lots of short sections in your documents—
  each requiring an analysis and conclusion.

Numbers

Ah, numerical structures. You have to love them. Whether listing
steps or times, when you reach the last item, the piece is done. If
you do need to round out your sequence and signal the end is
near, you can simply insert an "and," "or," or "finally" before the
last element. For the most part though, it goes this way:

1. Reports

2. Proposals

3. Blogs

4. E-mails

5. Websites

Letter closings

With so many e-mails flying through cyberspace, people write
fewer and fewer letters. Still, they aren't gone yet. The endings are
formulaic: Tell the reader what you plan to do next and how they
can reach you. You might say:

*If I don't hear back from you by next week, I will assume the situation
has been resolved. If you have any questions in the meantime, please
e-mail.*

You may not feel your letter needs a closing, but include one
anyway. They're pretty much the professional fashion, much like
wearing a suit and tie.

And...Goodbye

I've enjoyed writing this; hope you enjoyed reading it, and that it helps your writing improve!

A Final Q&P Tell-All

Tell all—tell everything—all your writing cares, concerns, and secrets, no matter what they are. And let me know if it's okay to post. Here's the address one last time:

www.quickandpainlessbusinesswriting.com.

Index

A

acronym, 41
active voice, 36, 114, 121-138
adages, pre-nitty-gritty, 12
ADHD, 23, 68
adjectives, 61
    endless, 62
    using before nouns, 83
adverbs, 85-86
advice, overdosing on, 11
agreement, tense, 74
Ali, Mohammad, 12
alpha noun, 36
Amazon.com, 40

*American Heritage Book of
    English Usage, The*, 97
analysis and support, 195
androgyny mistakes, 58
articles, 51
Associated Press Stylebook, 28
Atlantic monthly, 40
Attention Deficit
    Hyperactivity Disorder, 23
audience factor, the, 167

B

Baby Boomers, 22
beta noun, 35

Blackberries, 22, 27
Boston Globe, 40
bullets,
    facts about, 199
    misuse of, 200
    using, 108

C

CH2M HILL, 39-40
cheat sheet
    adverb, 87
    agreement, 74
    article, 54
    conjunction, 90
    general–specific, 45
    general–specific adjective, 64
    helping/linking verb, 85
    metaphor, 80
    noun reminder, 34
    possessive pronoun, 61
    preposition, 93
    pronoun, 60
    show don't tell, 147
Chicago Manual of Style, The, 28
Chronicle of Higher Education, 162
chronological order,
    198-199, 201
Churchill, Winston, 97
clause,
    dependent, 104-105
    independent, 104-105
clichés, 152
Clinton administration, 39, 113
Clinton, Bill, 41, 118
Clinton, Hillary, 158
cloning, 137
coaches, using, 13
comma splices, 109

communications, spoken, 140
comparative order, 198-199, 203
complete
    predicate, 23
    sentences, 104
Composition 101, 25
compound sentences, 104
compound–complex
    sentences, 105
concise, being 130
concise word use, 114
conclusions, 212
conjunction
    consumption, 95
    functions, 89-90
conjunctions, 89
    buried, 96
content
    unnecessary, 134
    using reliable, 116
contrasting order, 198-199, 203
cousin it, 126
cubicle, writing in your, 11
customer service, 21

D

delay, cost of, 20
dependent clause, 104-105
descriptive
    openings, 193
    order, 198-199, 202
diagramming sentences, 33
Disney, 27
documents, common, 21
Donald Duck, 27
double negatives, 27
drag queen, word use, 123
Dryden, John, 97

E

education, 23
English as a second language, 158
excited tone, 167
expressions, tired, 152

F

facts about your reader, 22
FANBOYS, 90
Federal, capitalization of, 39
federal government, 39, 114, 127, 200
feedback, sources of, 13
Ferguson, Miss, 23, 24, 34, 114, 153, 185
first
    line, importance of the, 145
    paragraph, importance of the, 145
formal tone, 165
Freud, Sigmund, 174
fun factor, remember the, 15

G

genderless action plan, 47-48
genderless-ness, 45-47
Glass, Philip, 100
glossary, using a, 42
glue words, 89
gold star, your (a), 57
Gore, Al, 118
Grammar and Composition, 185
grammar, definition of, 26
grammar
    gene, 26
    rules, 25

Grammar Mavens, 29, 41, 79, 95-96, 115
Gregorian chant, 100

H

Handbook of Nonsexist Writing, 47
help, asking for, 13
Hemingway, Ernest, 174
humorous tone, 168
hyper-formal tone, 165

I

iceberg theory of writing, Hemingway's, 174
imperative, the, 101
independent clause, 104-105
industry terminology, 160
infinitive, split an, 28
informal
    language, 140
    tone, 165
Information Technology Jargon Monitor, 162
information,
    obvious, 133
    read to get, 19
initiative on plain language, 39, 113, 118
instructions, writing, 21
introductory
    element, 122
    paragraphs, 192
I-phobia, 54
its—it's conundrum, 57
ivory tower, the, 24

J

Jargon Watch, 158
jargon
    as a tone-wrecker, 158
    your boss insists on, 30
Joplin, Janis, 33
Journalism.org, 14

L

language
    fashion, 27
    shifts, 45
Leave It to Beaver, 22
letter closings, 213
linking verbs, 83-85
listing, 179-182

M

manager, using your, 13
marketers, 124
marketing writing, 140
mass anonymity, 141
me-phobia, 55
message,
    a rag-tag, 186
    optimize your, 174
    subliminal, 174
metaphors, 79
    official, 81
    opening, 193
misplaced modifiers, 107
monotony, 100
Mothers Against Drunk
    Driving, 41
Ms. dilemma, the, 47
myself and I syndrome, the, 57

N

National Public Radio, 48
negatives, double, 27
New York Times, The, 13, 118, 144
noun, 34-36
    alpha, 36
    beta, 35
    naked, 41
    using bullets with, 38
noun
    nuggets, 37, 44
    uppers, 39
noun–verb marriage, 73
NPR, 48-49
numerical structures, 213

O

object of a sentence, 35
obstacles, overcoming, 12
Online Writing Lab, 53
openings,
    questions in, 194
    quotes in, 194
order imposing, 194
overgeneralization, avoiding, 136
overviews, 191

P

page requirements, 24
paragraph
    length, 198
    myths, 185-209
    structure, 182, 186
paragraph–brick connection, 186
passive voice, 36-37,
    123-126, 141

passives,
   eliminate all, 128
   problem, 125
peer editors, using, 13
perspective, getting, 12
phrases, 106
plain language, 39, 113-
   119, 200
   controversy about, 113
poet, becoming a, 33
policy decisions, 135
poor training, 24
positioning,
   aspects of, 176
   power, 145
power positioning, 145
practice makes perfect, 15
pre-paragraph, the, 188
preamble, lengthy, 29
prepositions, 89, 92
   problems with, 95
   ending a sentence with,
      27, 96
preposition past, 97
pronouns as rule breakers, 54
proposals, 136
protocol, word, 188
pseudo-words, 124
Pulitzer Prize, 13
Purdue University, 53
pyramid, the inverted, 195

Q

questions in openings, 194
quotes in openings, 194

R

Radner, Gilda, 89
reader profile, 22

reader-focus, 114, 139-155
reality checks, 19-30, 182
Red Bull, 24
response,
   getting the right, 20, 79
   getting the wrong, 21
   write to get a, 19
Russian tragedies, 14

S

Schoolhouse Rock, 90
Seagal, Steven, 27
second person, 140
seducing, 173
sensitive tone, 167
sentence
   length, 99-100
   types, 101-102
sentences,
   complex, 104
   compound, 104
sequential order, 201
serious tone, 168
Sesame Street, 26
show don't count, 147-151
show don't tell, 146
small-word buildup, 130
spinning, 173-175
split infinitive, 26, 28
spoken communications, 140
Star Trek, 28
State of the News Media report, 14
strategy, 13
   metaphor, 79
structure,
   creating a cohesive, 114
   how to control, 178-179
   the importance of, 173
Strunk and White, 12
Students Against Destructive
   Decisions, 41

Students Against Drunk
   Driving, 41
style–content connection, 137
subject lines, 189
subjunctive, 23
subliminal message, 174
summaries, 190, 212

T

taboo, words that are, 12
tax dollars, 118
tense,
   past, 69
   perfect, 71
   present, 70
   simple, 70
tense agreement, 74
than, then vs., 91
The Elements of Style, 12
then/than debate, 91
threshold, reader's energy, 66
tired expressions, 152
tone, 157-169
   conversational, 165
   excited, 167
   formal, 165
   humorous, 168
   hyper-formal, 165
   informal, 165
   sensitive, 167
   serious, 168
   using an accessible, 114
transitions, using, 187

U

uncertain volume, 141
un-paragraph, the, 206
usage, definition of, 26

V

variety–spice equation, 187
verb
   power, harnessing, 67
   tense, 68
verbs, 65-87
   action, 66, 82
   auxiliary, 158
   continuous tense, 71
   future tense, 70
   good guy, 69
   helping, 84
   hidden, 123
   linking, 66, 82-85
   past tense, 69
   perfect tense, 71
   present tense, 70
   simple tense, 70
voice,
   active, 36, 114, 121-138
   passive, 36-37, 141
volume, uncertain, 141

W

Wall Street Journal, The, 118
White House initiative on
   plain language, 39, 113, 118
White House, the, 39, 42, 113
White, E.B., 12
who/whom debate, 27, 61
womyn, 46
Woods, Tiger, 12
word protocol, 188
workplace documents,
   adopting the style of, 15

About the Author

Susan Benjamin has brought communications issues to the nation for almost 20 years. Publications from *The Wall Street Journal* to *The Chicago Tribune* have featured Susan's novel approaches while her opinion pieces on language-related issues have appeared in *USA Today*, *The Philadelphia Inquirer*, *The New York Daily News*, *Government Executive* and countless others. Her other books include *Instant Marketing for Almost Free* (Source Books, January, 2007) and *Words at Work, Business Writing in Half the Time with Twice the Power* (Perseus, 1997).

As a speaker, Susan has appeared on CNN and National Public Radio and other broadcasts. She has trained more than 100,000 federal and private sector employees in venues including videos, satellite broadcasts and in-class seminars; has given keynote and other addresses; and developed writing programs—virtual and face-to-face—for audiences worldwide. Her clients include the Carnegie

Mellon Executive Program, the National Geospacial-Intelligence Agency, Liberty Mutual Insurance Group, the Social Security Administration, and many others.

A former professor of literature and writing, Susan mentored academics at Harvard University and MIT. She participated in the White House Initiative on Plain Language under the Clinton administration, overseeing the revision of countless documents affecting millions of citizens each year. Her clients included the State Department, Department of Defense, Food and Drug Administration, and hundreds of private sector organizations.

Susan's research includes assessments of organizational communication processes and studies on how language affects reader-responsiveness. Among other results, her research helped the U.S. government overhaul their recruitment and hiring processes and the Treasury Department validate their approach to conveying regulatory requirements. Susan's articles about these findings have appeared in numerous publications including *Scribes Legal Journal*, *Government Executive*, and *Employment Management Today*.

Susan studied philosophy and writing at Boston University and Bennington College. She received her Masters in Writing from Lesley College where she worked with C. Michael Curtis, Senior Editor of *The Atlantic*.